This book is from
the kitchen library of

_____

# Mr. Food®'s
## Old World Cooking
## Made Easy

ALSO BY ART GINSBURG, MR. FOOD®

The Mr. Food® Cookbook, **"OOH IT'S SO GOOD!!™"** (1990)

Mr. Food® Cooks Like Mama (1992)
Mr. Food® Cooks Chicken (1993)
Mr. Food® Cooks Pasta (1993)
Mr. Food® Makes Dessert (1993)
Mr. Food® Cooks Real American (1994)
Mr. Food®'s Favorite Cookies (1994)
Mr. Food®'s Quick and Easy Side Dishes (1995)
Mr. Food® Grills It All in a Snap (1995)
Mr. Food®'s Fun Kitchen Tips and Shortcuts (and Recipes, Too!) (1995)
"Help, Mr. Food®! Company's Coming!" (1995)

# Mr. Food®'s
# OLD WORLD
# COOKING
# MADE EASY

# Art Ginsburg
## Mr. Food®

WILLIAM MORROW AND COMPANY, INC.

New York

Library of Congress Cataloging-in-Publication Data

Ginsburg, Art.
    Mr. Food®'s old world cooking made easy / Art Ginsburg.
        p.   cm.
    Includes index.
    ISBN 0-688-13138-7 (hardcover)
    I.Cookery, International.    2. Quick and easy cookery.   I. Title.
TX725.A1G378    1995
641.59—dc20                                                              95-37043
                                                                         CIP

Printed in the United States of America

2   3   4   5   6   7   8   9   10

BOOK DESIGN BY MICHAEL MENDELSOHN/MM DESIGN 2000, INC.

Dedicated to my parents
Charlie and Jennie—
A perfect blend of the Old World
And the New World—

And to their namesakes
Caryl, Chuck, and Shayna
Who are such an important influence
in my life and my work today.

# Acknowledgments

Whew! I have so many people to thank! I loved doing this book because it gave me the chance to find out more about family foods from far and near. And I'm so thankful to all the people of varied backgrounds who've shared family recipes and memories with me, and to our ancestors who were the creators of so many of the dishes we enjoy today. I have thanks, too, for the chefs in our ethnic and Old World restaurants and the home cooks who continue to pass down these wonderful traditional tastes to us all.

I want to express my appreciation to my daughter, Caryl Ginsburg Gershman, and to Howard Rosenthal for their commitment to making this a fun, informative book full of easy-to-make homestyle recipes. And, speaking of recipes, I've got a dynamite bunch of cooks who help me create and test these recipes—Patty Rosenthal, Alice Palombo, Monique Drummond, Fred Ritter, and Joe Peppi. Thanks to their persistence, we've come up with quick, tasty, winning versions of Old World recipes that work every time!

Thanks also to Ethel, Steve, and Carol Ginsburg, Laura Ratcliff, Laurie Carmusin, and Roy Fantel for their assistance and input. Then there's the rest of the supportive **Mr. Food**® team, and my encouraging agent, Bill Adler, my energetic publicist, Phyllis Heller, and the super creative team at William Morrow led by Al Marchioni. I appreciate all of their hard work and enthusiasm.

Once again I get to express my appreciation to companies, organizations, and individuals who've helped out by providing information and product suggestions:

American Spice Trade Association

Dairy Management Inc.

Entenmann's

Chef Mitchell Fantel of the New York Restaurant School

Heritage Clock Shop of Pompano Beach, Florida

Jana Brands, makers of frozen seafood products

M. E. Heuck Co., makers of Firm Grip™ kitchen tools

McCormick®/Schilling®

The McIlhenny Company, makers of Tabasco® Pepper Sauce

The National Beef Cooking Contest

The National Beef Council

The National Broiler Council

National Yiddish Book Center, South Hadley, Massachusetts

Pace Foods

Rabbi Charles Sherman, Temple Adath Yeshuran, Syracuse, New York

Ceil Spangelet

Syracuse University Department of Languages, Literatures, and Linguistics

Tryson House, makers of flavor sprays

# Contents

# Introduction

Recently I went to a Chinese restaurant that has an open kitchen . . . and it hit me! No, not the kitchen—the idea! There it was, all around me—the blend of old and new. With the combination of incredible aromas—of garlic, ginger, and sizzling wok cooking—and the teamwork of the family that was making and serving our meals, I knew I was experiencing the knowledge and customs of generations of Chinese cooks. I could taste the pride that had gone into preparing my food that night, and right then I knew I had to write a book that would capture a world of flavors and traditions. I set out to find ways to help people continue to experience the rich tastes of the Old World in ways that fit our new lifestyles.

Our great-grandmothers and grandmothers, our "bubbes," often took hours to prepare a single dish. And boy, do we remember how flavorful their cooking was! Sure, that's our prize when foods and flavorings have hours to "marry." But today most of us don't have that much time for cooking. So how can we keep from losing those great recipes and mouth-watering tastes forever? Read on!

I've come up with lots of shortcuts for our old family favorites. They're dishes from around the world. And now they're so easy that you'll be able to make them any time, not just on holidays! I say they're from the Old World, since almost everyone in this country has roots in some other place, too. I didn't have room for something from *every* country in the world. I've selected a mixture of my own favorites and other popular dishes that can be made from readily available ingredients. I'm sure you'll find lots of recipes here that you'll want to make over and over.

There are so many wonderful cuisines to experience! Each one has foods and flavorings that are particular to it, and there are many reasons for that. For example, climate is responsible for rice being dominant in Chinese dishes and potatoes so widely used in Irish ones. And because of location, we see lots more fish in Japanese cooking than in Swiss. Then there's religion. It has played a big role in the foods of different cultures. For people who don't cook on the Sabbath, for instance, hearty dishes are especially popular—ones often made with meats that can withstand hours of slow cooking started a day or two before they're to be eaten. And within religious groups and cultures where eating beef is forbidden, we often find that lamb and poultry dishes are more prevalent.

Then there are some basic differences in food preparation. For example, in some cultures it's more popular to prepare whole chickens, while others generally cut their chickens into small pieces for quick stir-frying. In America today we've come to think of a salad as a tossed green salad, but in the Middle East you usually find salads made of a variety of chopped vegetables (see Israeli Chopped Salad, page 38).

When people move away from the countries where they were born, their foods begin to show the influence of a cultural crossover. And since you know I always encourage you to experiment, why not try combining *your* favorite foods, spices, and cooking methods from a variety of cultures? Maybe top Neighborly Greek Chicken (page 118) with a rich Italian marinara sauce, or serve Shrimp Málaga (page 141) tossed with lo mein noodles (or vermicelli) for a spicy Chinese-style dish. It's easy—and it's another way for you to create more tasty dishes for your gang!

Most Americans think of Italian food as using lots of olive oil and tomatoes. Actually, that's *southern* Italian food—it's more Mediter-

ranean than northern Italian food, which is closer to French in that it uses lots of butter, cream, and, of course, wine. So you see, not only does each country have its own unique foods but so do different regions within countries. That's why I think we should all be open-minded about trying new foods and new combinations. If we say we don't like the food of a particular country, we could be missing out on something we'd really enjoy, since flavorings may vary greatly from one part of a country to another.

Speaking of flavorings, I've included an herb and spice chart (pages xxvi–xxxiii) that describes lots of different ones and also tells where each comes from. Knowing where herbs and spices come from helps us understand why different cultures flavor their foods the way they do. I've also included a chart of common food names and terms (pages xvi–xxv). It's interesting, and I'm sure it'll help explain words you may have heard before, as well as come in handy when you're looking for ways to add excitement to your everyday meals.

Unfortunately for our ancestors, they could make only what they could grow and raise themselves. They ate what was available. But advances in agriculture and transportation mean that today we can bring foods from around the world to our own tables. We can all enjoy New Zealand kiwifruit, Mexican hot peppers, and, of course, the always-in-demand Colombian coffee. Microwave ovens may be a relatively new invention, but for centuries Asian cooks have known how to cook quickly—in woks—while Indian cooks used tandoors (earthen ovens). For preserving food in the days before refrigeration, food was either dried, salted, pickled, or smoked. The tastes of those foods are what we want to preserve for now and the future.

So give these recipes a try—and turn your kitchen into an international food festival! Maybe serve the football gang African Chicken Wings (page 128), fill your family's bowls with Chinatown Hot 'N' Sour Soup (page 21) one night, make Shortcut Moussaka (page 75) the next night, and serve Crêpes Suzette (page 228) for brunch or dessert. And when you're looking for "a little something" to have with your coffee or tea, why not whip up some Pull-Apart Polish Babka (page 52)?

You're in for a world of easy favorites full of
**"OOH IT'S SO GOOD!!™"**

# Charts and Information

## Talking the Same Language: A Helpful Chart of Popular Food Terms

How many times have you heard foreign words and phrases used to describe foods and wondered where they came from? A lot of us even use these words without knowing what they really mean. I've included some of the more common ones here. You're probably already making lots of these foods. So why not make this a learning experience (it's great for the kids!) and give some new names to your everyday foods—maybe do it with your "go-alongs" each night—and let everyone think you've become an international chef!

| | |
|---|---|
| **À la bordelaise** | A brown sauce made with red wine, shallots, pepper, and thyme (originally made with red wine from Bordeaux, France—that's how it got its name) |
| **À la Provençale** | A dish containing tomatoes, onions, bell peppers, garlic, and herbs |
| **Al dente** | Means "to the tooth" in Italian and refers to pasta that has been cooked to the point where it has only a slight bit of uncooked core (giving you pasta with something to chew!) |
| **Aspic** | A jellied dish or jellied glaze |
| **Au gratin** | A baked dish most commonly topped with crumbs and cheese, and top-browned |

| | |
|---|---|
| **Au jus** | Served with natural juices, drippings, or gravy |
| **Babka** | Polish for "grandmother," but also refers to a yeast cake made with nuts and raisins; popular year-round but especially at the Easter holidays (see Pull-Apart Polish Babka, page 52) |
| **Baklava** | A Greek dessert made of stacked crisp layers of butter-brushed phyllo pastry sheets with walnut filling and soaked with honey syrup (see Not-Traditional Baklava, page 218) |
| **Beurre** | French for "butter" |
| **Bisque** | Usually refers to a thick soup made from shellfish |
| **Bon appétit** | Literally means "good appetite" and is said when wishing for someone to enjoy their meal |
| **Borscht** | A Ukrainian or Russian beet soup made with meat and/or cabbage and vegetables (see Beefy Russian Borscht, page 25, and Chilled Beet Borscht, page 32) |
| **Braten** | A German marinated pot roast usually cooked in a small amount of liquid on the stovetop (see New Sauerbraten, page 105) |
| **Bratwurst** | A German-style sausage that is typically pan-fried |
| **Burrito** | A soft flour tortilla wrapped around a meat, chicken, cheese, or bean filling |
| **Calzone** | An Italian turnover stuffed with ingredients that you'd find on pizza (see Pizza Calzones, page 77) |
| **Canapé** | An appetizer of a small piece of toasted or fried bread topped with a flavorful spread and, typically, garnished |

| | |
|---|---|
| **Cappuccino** | A very strong coffee made with hot steamed milk and often served with a liqueur and/or cinnamon (see Cappuccino Dessert, page 208) |
| **Carne** | Spanish for "meat," as in the dish chili con carne |
| **Caviar** | The roe (eggs) of sturgeon and salmon; considered a delicacy and usually pricey |
| **Cholent** | A long-cooked Israeli stew made with beef, potatoes, barley, and beans |
| **Chorizo** | A Spanish type of pork sausage that's made with paprika (which gives it its bright red color) |
| **Cilantro** | The fresh form of coriander, this leafy flavoring is popular in Spanish and Latin cooking; as ground coriander, it's used in many Near and Middle Eastern foods |
| **Compote** | Usually refers to a stew of fresh or dried fruit in a thick syrup |
| **Coquilles** | French for "seashells" (see Homestyle Coquilles St.-Jacques, page 135) |
| **Couscous** | A pasta-like grain made from wheat (see Chicken and Couscous, page 127) |
| **Crème** | French for "cream" |
| **Crêpe** | A thin French pancake usually folded or wrapped around any savory or sweet filling (see Crêpes Suzette, page 228) |
| **Croissant** | A crescent-shaped French pastry roll with rich, flaky, buttery layers |

| | |
|---|---|
| **Croutons** | Small cubes of plain or seasoned bread that are toasted or fried; usually served as a topping for soups and tossed salads |
| **Crudités** | A selection of cut fresh raw or blanched vegetables served as an hors d'oeuvre with dipping sauces |
| **Demitasse** | French for "half a cup," this usually refers to a small cup of strong black coffee |
| **Diablo/diavolo** | Spanish and Italian, respectively, for "devil"; usually refers to a spicy-hot dish |
| **Dim sum** | Steamed dumplings or buns usually filled with ground meats, seafood, or poultry and vegetables; also other Chinese appetizers, this often refers to many different types served together, making a complete meal |
| **Du jour** | French for "of the day"; usually refers to a restaurant's daily special |
| **Éclair** | An oblong-shaped pastry filled with custard or whipped cream and topped with a chocolate glaze or icing |
| **En brochette** | Something served and/or cooked on a skewer; typically refers to a kebab (see Greek Lamb Kebabs, page 67) |
| **En papillote** | Refers to a cooking method where food is wrapped and baked in a parchment paper casing |
| **Entrée** | In the United States, this generally refers to the main course of a meal |
| **Falafel** | Small fried fritter made of ground garbanzo beans (chick peas) and typically served on pita bread (see Easy Falafels, page 9) |

| **Filet, fillet** | Long, thin piece of boneless meat, like filet mignon; or long, thin piece of boneless fish or chicken |
| **Five-spice powder** | A popular Chinese spice combination of ground fennel, cloves, Szechuan peppercorns, star anise, and cinnamon |
| **Flambé(e)** | French for "blaze" and refers to food served with a liqueur or spirit poured over and lighted for dramatic effect while serving; **not recommended to be done at home!** (see Crêpes Suzette, page 228) |
| **Flan** | A light egg custard (similar to Crème Caramel, page 220) |
| **Florentine** | A food preparation using spinach |
| **Fondue** | From the French word for "melt," it refers to a melted cheese or chocolate mixture that is served with foods to be dipped in it using long-handled forks or skewers |
| **Foo yung** | A Chinese omelet made with meat, fish, or vegetables (see Shrimp Egg Foo Yung, page 139) |
| **Fraise** | French for "strawberry" (and fraises are perfect for dipping in chocolate fondue, as mentioned above!) |
| **Frappé** | A semifrozen beverage |
| **Fromage** | French for "cheese" |
| **Gorgonzola** | A very strong Italian blue cheese (Mmm . . . one of my favorites!) |
| **Goulash** | A thick meat stew (see my shortcut version, Hungarian Goulash Soup, page 22) |
| **Gravlax** | Thinly sliced Swedish salmon cured with salt, pepper, sugar, and dill |

| | |
|---|---|
| **Hoisin sauce** | A popular Chinese sauce used for marinating, cooking, and dipping; made from garlic, hot peppers, soy beans, and spices (try some with Chinese Chicken Bites, page 2) |
| **Hummus** | A spread or dip made of ground garbanzo beans (chick peas) (see Middle Eastern Dip, page 17) |
| **Jambon** | French for "ham" |
| **Jardinière** | From the French word for "garden," it refers to a selection of mixed vegetables |
| **Julienne** | Matchstick-size cut vegetables or meats |
| **Kasha** | Roasted buckwheat, a grain popular in Russian cooking that is often cooked with mushrooms and onions (see Great-Grandma's Kasha, page 168) |
| **Kielbasa** | A spicy beef and pork Polish sausage; today there are kosher varieties as well as lighter versions made with chicken and turkey (see All-in-One Kielbasa, page 89) |
| **Knödel** | German dumpling |
| **Lavash** | A thin, crispy white bread that's used today like crackers |
| **Legume** | French for "vegetable"; in English it refers mostly to dried peas and beans |
| **Lyonnaise** | Cooked with onions (see So-Easy Potatoes Lyonnaise, page 158) |
| **Maison** | French for "house," a term usually used when referring to a restaurant's dish that's the specialty of the house |

**Marzipan**    A firm, pliable paste of finely ground almonds, confectioners' sugar, and corn syrup that can be rolled out like a pie dough and is often molded into flowers and shapes for decorating fancy pastries and cakes

**Mein**    Chinese for "noodles" (see Better-Than-Ever Lo Mein, page 172)

**Meringue**    Egg whites whipped with sugar to the stiff peak stage and usually made into cookies or as a pie topping (the most familiar examples are lemon meringue pie and baked Alaska)

**Moussaka**    A Greek baked dish consisting of layers of eggplant and ground beef topped with a white sauce or a custard (see Shortcut Moussaka, page 75)

**Mousse**    A light dish made with whipped cream and flavorings, usually made in a mold and served chilled or frozen (see Almost-Belgian Chocolate Mousse, page 234)

**Nachos**    A Mexican-style appetizer of tortilla chips, chilies, and melted cheese; today it's popular made also with olives, scallions, and other vegetables

**Oeuf**    French for "egg"

**Paella**    A flavorful Spanish stew most often made with chicken, seafood, vegetables, and rice

**Pain**    French for "bread"

**Pâté**    Ground fish, meat, or poultry that is baked and served chilled as an appetizer

**Pâté de foie gras**    A paste of goose liver served as an appetizer

**Pâtisserie**    French for "pastry shop" (and boy, the French sure are known for their great pastries!)

| | |
|---|---|
| **Pesto** | A sauce of fresh basil, olive oil, garlic, pine (or other) nuts, and grated Parmesan or Romano cheese |
| **Phyllo dough** | Very thin, delicate pastry layers, often found in Greek dishes |
| **Pièce de résistance** | Refers to a very special main-dish food—one that usually can't be resisted |
| **Pomme** | French for "apple" |
| **Pomme de terre** | French for "potato" (literally means "apple of the earth") |
| **Potage** | French for "soup" (for one of my favorite French soups, try Fast French Onion Soup, page 29) |
| **Poulet** | French for "chicken" (check out all the great *poulet* recipes I've got for you) |
| **Prosciutto** | A dried, cured spicy ham (usually quite pricey!) |
| **Purée** | Refers to food that has been mashed until almost liquefied |
| **Quiche** | A savory pie made with cream, cheese, and vegetables and/or seafood or meats |
| **Ragoût** | A thick, highly seasoned stew |
| **Ratatouille** | A mixed vegetable dish that usually includes eggplant, tomatoes, and garlic and is served either warm or cold |
| **Risotto** | Italian-style rice cooked in broth and, usually, served with cheese (see Ready-in-Minutes Risotto, page 164) |
| **Roux** | A cooked mixture of butter and flour used to thicken soups and sauces |
| **Sake** | Japanese rice wine |

| | |
|---|---|
| **Sauté** | To lightly pan- or skillet-fry foods in a small amount of fat over high heat |
| **Schnapps** | A strong dry liquor available in fruit and other flavors |
| **Schnitzel** | Very thin boneless fillet of sautéed veal, pork, or beef (see my updated version made with chicken, Chicken "Schnitzel" with Mushroom Sauce, page 125) |
| **Smörgåsbord** | Originally referred to a selection of Scandinavian foods, but now refers to any type of hot and cold food served on a buffet table |
| **Soufflé** | A delicate baked custard that "puffs up" during baking; contains anything from cheese or meat to chocolate |
| **Taco** | A crispy or soft corn tortilla wrapped around a filling of meat, chicken, cheese, or beans |
| **Tempura** | A lightly battered deep-fried Japanese dish of poultry, seafood, or vegetables, usually served with a selection of dipping sauces |
| **Tortilla** | A thin corn pancake |
| **Truffle** | A fancy edible fungus used for seasoning and garnishing (usually quite pricey!); also, a chocolate truffle is a rich chocolate confection often shaped like the edible fungus |
| **Tutti-frutti** | Mixed fruits |
| **Véronique** | Made with grapes (see Grapevine Sole, page 149) |
| **Vichyssoise** | A cream soup made of potatoes and chicken stock that is usually served chilled |
| **Vinaigrette** | A salad dressing or marinade of oil, vinegar, herbs, and spices |

# International Herbs and Spices

Boy, oh boy, do I love my seasonings! They give all our foods personality and zing. We've got a world of flavors right on our spice shelves at the supermarket and at home, and I bet lots of you don't even know what a great collection of Old World favorites you already have. I try to include interesting seasonings and combinations in my recipes, while keeping them simple and offering substitution suggestions whenever possible. I want you to be comfortable and not intimidated by my recipes. So go ahead and experiment—maybe use dried basil one time and dill the next, try some fresh herbs, and before you know it, you'll be creating great new versions of your regular dishes! Here's a good starting point for information about the most popular herbs and spices. (Shake 'em up—everybody can use it once in a while!)

| Herb or Spice | Descriptions and Usage | Major Sources |
|---|---|---|
| **Allspice** (spice) | Clove-like flavor, but smoother and mellower | Jamaica, Honduras, Mexico, Guatemala |
| **Anise seed** (herb seed) | Licorice-like flavor; from the parsley family, its oil is used for licorice flavoring | Turkey, Spain |
| **Basil** (herb) | Bright green leaves most often used to enhance tomato dishes; currently enjoying the fastest popularity growth of an herb | U.S., Egypt, France |

| Herb or Spice | Descriptions and Usage | Major Sources |
|---|---|---|
| **Bay leaves** (herb) | Large, olive-green leaves; the only dried herb to come in its original, whole leaf form | Turkey |
| **Black peppercorns** (spice) | The whole dried berry (peppercorn) is used for ground black pepper | Indonesia, India, Brazil, Malaysia |
| **Caraway seed** (herb seed) | Hard, brown seeds that are in "seeded" rye bread; a favorite flavor addition for sauerkraut, too | Netherlands, Egypt, Poland |
| **Cardamom seed** (spice) | Dark brown seeds used in Scandinavian baked goods and Indian foods; its biggest use is in Middle Eastern coffee | Guatemala, India, Costa Rica |
| **Celery seed** (herb seed) | Tiny brown seeds with a strong celery flavor, heavily used in salad dressings, sauces, and vegetable cocktails | India, People's Republic of China |
| **Chervil** (herb) | Much like parsley, but sweeter and more aromatic with an anise-like fragrance and a slight pepper flavor | France, U.S. |

| Herb or Spice | Descriptions and Usage | Major Sources |
| --- | --- | --- |
| **Chili pepper** (spice) | Available in many sizes and shapes and used fresh or dried (ground or flaked) to add powerful flavor (from sweet to spicy hot) to foods | U.S., Mexico |
| **Chives** (herb) | A member of the onion family with tubular green leaves; normally freeze-dried to protect its fragile quality and vibrant green color | U.S. |
| **Cinnamon** (Cassia) (spice) | Reddish brown with a strong flavor, in the U.S. it's the more popular of two main types | Indonesia, People's Republic of China, Taiwan |
| **Cloves** (spice) | Its unusual nail-like shape makes it an exotic garnish; ground cloves have a very strong flavor | Brazil, Madagascar, Tanzania, Indonesia, Sri Lanka |
| **Coriander seed** (herb seed) | Small, round, buff-colored seeds that have a mild, delicately fragrant aroma with a lemony/sage undertone | Morocco, Romania, Argentina, Egypt |
| **Cumin seed** ("comino") (herb seed) | Small, elongated, yellowish-brown seeds that add an aromatic flavor to chili powder and curries | Turkey, People's Republic of China, Pakistan, India |

| Herb or Spice | Descriptions and Usage | Major Sources |
|---|---|---|
| **Dill seed** (herb seed) | Small, oval-shaped, tan seed that's the principal flavor of dill pickles; also used in dips, sauces, and sausages | India, Pakistan |
| **Dillweed** (herb) | Green, feathery leaves of the dill plant; used in sauces for fish, cheese dips, salads, and dressings | U.S., Egypt |
| **Fennel seed** (herb seed) | Small, yellowish-brown seeds with an anise-like flavor; the distinctive flavor in Italian sausages (both sweet and hot) | India, Egypt |
| **Ginger** (spice) | Biting but sweet root that's used fresh (chopped or grated) or dried (powdered) for seasoning many different dishes, from pies to Asian dishes | People's Republic of China, Nigeria, India, Jamaica |
| **Green peppercorns** | The pepper berries are picked while still green, resulting in somewhat milder flavor than black peppercorns | Madagascar, India |

| Herb or Spice | Descriptions and Usage | Major Sources |
|---|---|---|
| **Mace** (spice) | Derived from the fibrous outer coating of the nutmeg seed, its flavor is stronger than nutmeg; ground mace is often used for light-colored baked products such as pound cake | Indonesia |
| **Marjoram** (herb) | A cousin of oregano, but with a milder, sweeter flavor | Egypt |
| **Mint flakes** (herb) | Dark green leaves of either the peppermint or spearmint plant; spearmint is the mint usually used for packaged mint flakes | U.S., Egypt |
| **Mustard seed** (spice) | Tiny yellow or brownish seeds of a member of the cabbage family: yellow (or white) seeds have a sharp bite, but no aromatic pungency; brown seeds are aromatically pungent as well as biting (i.e., Chinese restaurant mustard) | Canada, U.S. |
| **Nutmeg** (spice) | A brown seed usually used ground; an all-purpose spice found in all types of foods | Indonesia, West Indies |

| Herb or Spice | Descriptions and Usage | Major Sources |
|---|---|---|
| **Oregano** (herb) | Two distinct types: Mediterranean (used in Italian and Greek foods) and Mexican (used in Mexican and Tex-Mex foods) | Turkey, Mexico, Greece, Israel |
| **Paprika** (spice) | Its flavor can range from sweet-mild to mildly pungent and is an all-purpose spice found in all types of foods and often used for garnishing | U.S., Spain, Hungary |
| **Parsley** (herb) | With their bright green leaves and fresh taste, the two popular varieties are curly and Italian; used fresh or dried (flaked) in many types of foods and often for garnishing | U.S., Mexico, Israel |
| **Poppy seed** (herb seed) | Tiny, gray-blue seeds of the poppy plant; ideal for breads and pastries, and also popular in salads (the same plant produces opium and morphine, but the seeds have no drug significance) | Netherlands, Australia, Turkey |

| Herb or Spice | Descriptions and Usage | Major Sources |
|---|---|---|
| **Red pepper** (spice) | Also known as cayenne pepper, it refers to the dried fruit (pods) of various small, hot peppers that are usually ground and used for adding a flavorful "zing" to foods | Pakistan, People's Republic of China, Mexico, India, Turkey |
| **Rosemary** (herb) | Green, needle-like leaves often teamed with lamb, but also important in Italian herb blends, sauces, and salad dressings | Yugoslavia, Portugal |
| **Saffron** (herb) | By the pound, our most expensive spice, but a pinch does so much flavoring and coloring that it goes a long way | Spain, Portugal |
| **Sage** (herb) | Available "cut," "rubbed," and "ground," and used in poultry dishes and pies; especially popular in the U.S. during autumn and winter holiday seasons | Yugoslavia, Albania, Turkey |
| **Savory** (herb) | A member of the mint family that's also in poultry seasoning and other herb blends and is especially good teamed with green beans | Yugoslavia, France |

| Herb or Spice | Descriptions and Usage | Major Sources |
|---|---|---|
| **Sesame seed** ("benne") (herb seed) | Small, oval, pearly white seeds that need toasting or baking to develop their nutty flavor | Mexico, Guatemala, India, El Salvador, Honduras, People's Republic of China |
| **Star anise** (spice) | Anise-like flavor; old-time pickling favorite | People's Republic of China |
| **Tarragon** (herb) | Slender, dark green leaves distinctive for their hint of anise flavor; found in béarnaise sauce, salad dressings, and vinegars | France, U.S. |
| **Thyme** (herb) | Grayish-green leaves that are one of the strongest herbs; found in herb blends and in Manhattan-style clam chowder | Spain, Morocco |
| **Turmeric** (spice) | Orange colored roots that provide color for prepared mustards, curry powder, mayonnaise, sauces, pickles, and relishes | India, Costa Rica, People's Republic of China |
| **White peppercorns** | White pepper has the heat but not the total bouquet of black; often chosen for light-colored soups and sauces | Indonesia, Brazil |

Adapted from information provided by the American Spice Trade Association

# Measuring Up: Metric Weights and Measures

You know me—always trying to keep things simple. Well, when I was putting together all of these recipes from the Old World, I kept coming across ingredients that were listed in metric measurements. It's a decimal system of weights and measures that's based on units of ten. It uses the kilogram for dry weight, the liter for liquids, and the meter for length. When I asked some of my viewers and readers if they thought I should include a metric conversion chart in this book, their response was an overwhelming "Yes!" It's very likely that the U.S. system of measurements may eventually change to metrics so that we can be consistent with most of the rest of the world, so I figured that it's a good thing to include here . . . just in case. Even if you don't use this chart too often, it'll be a good thing to have at your fingertips if you *ever do* need it. Here it is . . . "for good measure"!

## Weights

| U.S. Measures | Metric Measures* |
|---|---|
| about 1 teaspoon | 5 grams |
| ¼ ounce | 7 grams |
| ⅓ ounce | 10 grams |
| ½ ounce | 14 grams |
| 1 ounce | 28 grams |
| 1¾ ounces | 50 grams |
| 2 ounces | 57 grams |

*Some metric equivalents are rounded for quick reference.

# Weights

| U.S. Measures | Metric Measures* |
|---|---|
| 3 ounces | 85 grams |
| 3½ ounces | 100 grams |
| 4 ounces (¼ pound) | 114 grams |
| 6 ounces | 170 grams |
| 8 ounces (½ pound) | 227 grams |
| 9 ounces | 250 grams |
| 16 ounces (1 pound) | 464 grams |
| 2 pounds 3¼ ounces | 1 kilogram (1,000 grams) |

# Fluid Measures

| U.S. Measures | Rounded Metric Measures* |
|---|---|
| ¼ teaspoon | 1 milliliter |
| ½ teaspoon | 2.5 milliliters |
| ¾ teaspoon | 3.7 milliliters |
| 1 teaspoon | 5 milliliters |
| 1 tablespoon (3 teaspoons) | 15 milliliters |
| 2 tablespoons (1 ounce) | 30 milliliters |
| ¼ cup | 60 milliliters |
| ⅓ cup | 80 milliliters |
| ½ cup | 120 milliliters |

*Some metric equivalents are rounded for quick reference.

*continued*

# Fluid Measures

| U.S. Measures | Rounded Metric Measures* |
|---|---|
| ⅔ cup | 160 milliliters |
| ¾ cup | 180 milliliters |
| 1 cup (8 ounces) | 240 milliliters |
| 1 cup plus 2¼ teaspoons | ¼ liter |
| 2 cups (1 pint) | 480 milliliters |
| 1 pint plus 4½ teaspoons | ½ liter |
| 3 cups | 720 milliliters |
| 4 cups (1 quart) plus 4 scant tablespoons | 1 liter |
| 4 quarts (1 gallon) | 3¾ liters |
| 2½ gallons plus about 2½ cups | 10 liters |

# Length

| U.S. Measures | Metric Measures* |
|---|---|
| ⅛ inch | 3 millimeters |
| ¼ inch | 6 millimeters |
| ⅜ inch | 1 centimeter |
| ½ inch | 1.2 centimeters |
| ¾ inch | 2 centimeters |
| 1 inch | 2.5 centimeters |

*Some metric equivalents are rounded for quick reference.

# Length

| U.S. Measures | Metric Measures |
| --- | --- |
| 1¼ inches | 3.1 centimeters |
| 1½ inches | 3.7 centimeters |
| 2 inches | 5 centimeters |
| 3 inches | 7.5 centimeters |
| 4 inches | 10 centimeters |
| 5 inches | 12.5 centimeters |
| 12 inches (1 foot) | 30 centimeters |
| 39⅓ inches | 1 meter |

*Some metric equivalents are rounded for quick reference.

# Temperatures

| Degrees Fahrenheit (F.) | Degrees Centigrade or Celsius (C.) |
| --- | --- |
| 32 (water freezes) | 0 |
| 212 (water boils) | 100 |
| 250 (low or slow oven) | 120 |
| 300 (medium-low oven) | 150 |
| 350 (medium or moderate oven) | 175 |
| 400 (hot oven) | 205 |
| 450 (very hot oven) | 232 |
| 500 (extremely hot oven) | 260 |

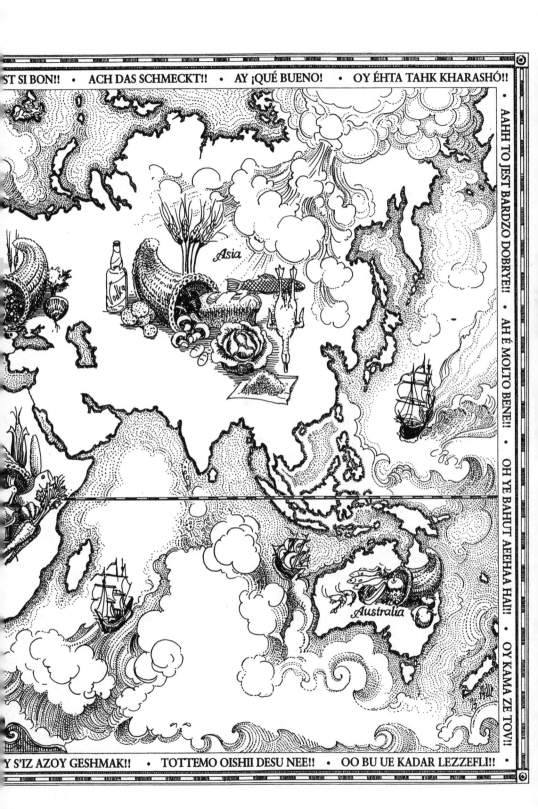

# Notes from Mr. Food®

## Lighten Up...with Food Sprays

Throughout this book, and in my other cookbooks, I frequently mention nonstick vegetable and baking sprays and recommend using them to coat cookware and bakeware before placing food in or on them. Here's why: These sprays are easy to use and, used as directed, they add no measurable amount of fat to our food, and now they're even available in nonaerosol *and* in flavored varieties! The flavored sprays are super ways to add a touch of taste, either before or after cooking foods, without adding lots of fat and calories.

## Serving Sizes

I like to serve generous portions myself, so I generally figure that way when I list the number of portions to expect from my recipes. Yes, appetites do vary and *you* know the special food loves of your eaters, so, as always, you be the judge of how much to make.

## Packaged Foods

Packaged food sizes may vary by brand. Generally, the sizes indicated in these recipes are average sizes. If you can't find the exact package size listed in the ingredients, whatever package is closest in size will usually do the trick.

# Generations of Appetizers

# Chinese Chicken Bites

*30 to 35 pieces*

*One of my favorite parts of going to a Chinese restaurant is the food we get before the main course! Now it's easy to make these at home to create our own appetizer poo-poo platter.*

1 pound ground chicken
3 to 4 scallions, finely chopped (about ½ cup)
2 tablespoons all-purpose flour
1 tablespoon soy sauce
1 tablespoon water
½ teaspoon sesame oil
¼ teaspoon ground ginger
1 teaspoon salt
½ teaspoon pepper
Peanut oil for frying

In a medium-sized bowl, combine all the ingredients except the peanut oil; mix well. Cover the bottom of a large skillet with about ½ inch peanut oil and heat over medium-high heat. Drop the chicken mixture by teaspoonfuls into the hot oil. Reduce the heat to medium-low and fry the chicken pieces for 5 to 6 minutes or until golden brown, turning once. Drain on paper towels and serve immediately.

NOTE: Serve these with hoisin sauce or your favorite Chinese dipping sauce. Why not try using ground turkey in place of the ground chicken? Go ahead—you'll get the same great taste.

# Swedish Meatballs

*30 to 35 meatballs*

*Did you know that the sour cream in this sauce makes these Swedish? (I thought it just made them yummy!)*

1¼ pounds ground beef
½ cup dry bread crumbs
1 egg
½ teaspoon onion powder
1½ teaspoons salt, divided
½ teaspoon pepper, divided
1 jar (12 ounces) brown gravy
½ cup sour cream
1 teaspoon Worcestershire sauce
½ teaspoon bottled browning and seasoning sauce

Preheat the oven to 375°F. In a medium-sized bowl, combine the ground beef, bread crumbs, egg, onion powder, 1 teaspoon salt, and ¼ teaspoon pepper; mix well. Form into 1-inch meatballs and place on a cookie sheet that has been coated with nonstick vegetable spray. Bake for 20 minutes or until the meatballs are cooked through. In a large saucepan, combine the remaining ingredients. Heat over medium-high heat until just bubbly. Add the meatballs and cook until heated through, about 5 minutes, stirring gently to coat the meatballs.

NOTE: These can be served over cooked noodles or rice and served as a main dish. Use lowfat or nonfat sour cream to help cut down on the fat, if you'd like.

# Swiss Fondue Bread

*2 cups*

*Everybody loves the taste of cheese fondue, but nobody likes the work and cleanup of making it the traditional way. Now you can have this Old World taste today-easy!*

⅓ cup mayonnaise
¼ cup dry white wine
2 tablespoons scallion rings
2 tablespoons Dijon-style mustard
2 cups (8 ounces) shredded Swiss cheese
1 loaf (1 pound) French or Italian bread, cut in half lengthwise

Preheat the oven to broil. In a medium-sized bowl, combine the mayonnaise, wine, scallion, and mustard; mix well. Stir in the Swiss cheese. Place the 2 halves of bread cut side up under the broiler and toast lightly. Remove from the oven and spread the cheese mixture evenly over each half. Return to the oven for 3 to 5 minutes or until the cheese is brown and bubbly.

NOTE: Wanna give this a bit more "zing"? Add ⅛ teaspoon dried dill, basil, oregano—or your favorite dried spice—to the cheese mixture.

# Quiche Lorraine

*6 to 8 servings*

*We've all seen quiche with lots of different fillings, but when it's accented with bacon this way, it's like our old French standby.*

1 cup (4 ounces) shredded Cheddar cheese
1 cup (4 ounces) shredded Swiss cheese
1 unbaked 9-inch pie shell
½ cup bacon bits
2 eggs
1 cup milk
1 teaspoon onion powder
¼ teaspoon pepper
¼ teaspoon ground nutmeg, for topping

*C'EST SI BON!!*
*PARIS*
*FRANCE*

Preheat the oven to 350°F. In a medium-sized bowl, combine the cheeses and sprinkle half the mixture into the pie shell. Sprinkle on the bacon bits, then cover with the remaining cheese combination. In a small bowl, combine the eggs, milk, onion powder, and pepper and beat until thoroughly mixed. Pour over the cheese and sprinkle with the nutmeg. Bake for 40 to 45 minutes or until firm and a wooden toothpick inserted in the center comes out clean. Cool for 5 minutes before cutting into pie-shaped slices.

NOTE: Go ahead—mix or match your favorite cheeses. This is even a great way to use up those bits of leftover cheeses in the back of your fridge.

# Today's Samosas

*26 to 30 pieces*

*Indian cooking of yesterday certainly has made its way into our hearts and bellies today ... and it's sure a lot easier now, too!*

½ cup raisins
½ pound ground beef
1 small onion, chopped (about ¾ cup)
2 teaspoons curry powder
¾ teaspoon ground cumin
¼ teaspoon garlic powder
⅛ teaspoon salt
⅛ teaspoon pepper
1 package (12 ounces) wonton skins (26 to 30 pieces)
1 egg, beaten
Nonstick vegetable spray

INDIA
oh ye bahut
aeehaa hai!
NEW DELH

Preheat the oven to 375°F. Soak the raisins in warm water for 10 minutes, then drain. Meanwhile, in a medium-sized skillet, sauté the beef and onion until browned. Drain off the fat, then add the drained raisins, curry, cumin, garlic, salt, and pepper; mix well. Moisten the edges of each wonton skin with the beaten egg, then spoon 1 teaspoon of the beef mixture into the center of each skin. Fold each skin in half to form a triangle and seal the edges. Place the samosas onto a cookie sheet that has been coated with nonstick vegetable spray and spray each one, coating evenly. Bake for 10 to 12 minutes or until the bottoms are golden and crisp.

NOTE: You can make these a day ahead and reheat them on a cookie sheet in a 300°F. oven for 12 to 15 minutes, or until hot.

# Quick Norwegian Herring

*8 servings*

*Herring can be found in recipes from so many different cultures, but I've found it to be most popular in Scandinavian countries. So, let me share a recipe from a Norwegian fan!*

1 jar (12 ounces) pickled cut herring fillets, drained and liquid
reserved
1 cup sour cream
1 cup thinly sliced onion
1 teaspoon dried dill
⅛ teaspoon pepper

In a medium-sized bowl, combine 4 tablespoons of the reserved herring liquid, the sour cream, onion, dill, and pepper; mix until smooth. Add the herring and toss to coat evenly. Cover and chill for about an hour to blend the flavors.

NOTE: Serve this with toothpicks as an appetizer, or maybe as a go-along with your green salad.

# Sicilian Pizza Roll-up

*4 to 6 servings*

*Who says pizza has to be flat? Not me! 'Cause when you roll it up and bake it, it becomes a pizza roll-up that's really easy to eat . . . so maybe you should make a double batch!*

1 pound ready-bake frozen bread dough, thawed
1 package (3 ounces) sliced pepperoni
1½ cups (6 ounces) shredded mozzarella cheese
¾ cup (one 7-ounce jar) roasted peppers, drained
½ teaspoon garlic powder
1 egg, beaten

Preheat the oven to 375°F. On a 10" × 15" cookie sheet that has been coated with nonstick vegetable spray, spread enough dough to cover the pan bottom. Place the pepperoni slices lengthwise on the dough, keeping them about 2 inches from the edges. Cover the pepperoni with the cheese, then the roasted peppers. Sprinkle with the garlic powder. Roll the dough lengthwise, pinching the seams together. Brush the top with the egg and bake seam side down for 35 to 40 minutes or until golden brown. Let cool for 5 minutes before slicing.

NOTE: Remember, there are no rules. Want to add some sliced mushrooms, cooked ground sausage, or even anchovies? Go ahead! It's *your* pizza!

# Easy Falafels

*20 pieces*

*When you want something different to serve the gang, try this Middle Eastern treat that's super as a before-dinner munchie or as a side dish. It's full of the great Old World flavors that we still love today.*

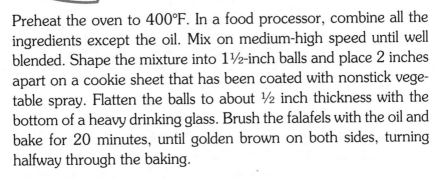

1 can (15 to 19 ounces) garbanzo beans (chick peas), drained
1 cup dry bread crumbs
2 eggs
2 tablespoons chopped fresh parsley
1 tablespoon olive oil
1 teaspoon lemon juice
1 teaspoon garlic powder
½ teaspoon salt
½ teaspoon pepper
½ teaspoon ground cumin
½ cup vegetable oil

Preheat the oven to 400°F. In a food processor, combine all the ingredients except the oil. Mix on medium-high speed until well blended. Shape the mixture into 1½-inch balls and place 2 inches apart on a cookie sheet that has been coated with nonstick vegetable spray. Flatten the balls to about ½ inch thickness with the bottom of a heavy drinking glass. Brush the falafels with the oil and bake for 20 minutes, until golden brown on both sides, turning halfway through the baking.

NOTE: Falafels are traditionally served in pita bread with chopped lettuce, tomato, and onion, and with tahini, a sesame sauce that can usually be found ready-made in the ethnic foods section of the supermarket.

# Sweet-and-Sour Teriyaki Wings

*8 to 10 servings*

*I love both sweet-and-sour and teriyaki flavors, so I figured I should try combining them... Wow! Wait till you taste the results!*

10 pounds chicken wingettes or drumettes or combination,
thawed if frozen
2 cups sweet-and-sour sauce
½ cup teriyaki sauce
¼ cup sesame seeds

Preheat the oven to 450°F. Lay out the chicken on cookie sheets that have been coated with nonstick vegetable spray. Bake the chicken for 20 minutes, then remove from the oven and drain any liquid. Combine the remaining ingredients in a large bowl. Place the chicken wings in the sauce and toss to coat well. Place the coated wings back on the cookie sheets and return them to the oven; cook for 25 minutes longer or until the glaze begins to caramelize and the chicken is cooked through.

NOTE: Sweet-and-sour sauce is often called duck sauce. They're almost interchangeable and can be found in the supermarket ethnic foods section. Taste may differ by brand, so if you like the sauce on the sweet side, you can add 1 to 2 tablespoons of brown sugar to it. If you like it spicy, you might want to add 2 to 3 dashes of hot pepper sauce.

# Grandma's Chopped Liver

*3 pounds*

*Here's the taste of Grandma's chopped liver without all the hard work. Is it possible? Yup, it is. And I betcha Grandma will want this recipe after she tastes it and finds out how easy it is!*

2 pounds beef or calf's liver steaks
½ cup vegetable oil
6 large onions, sliced
8 hard-boiled eggs, peeled
½ cup water
1 tablespoon sugar
2½ teaspoons salt
½ teaspoon pepper

Preheat the oven to 375°F. Place the liver on a rimmed cookie sheet and bake for 20 to 25 minutes or until no red remains. Meanwhile, heat the oil in a large skillet over medium-high heat. Add the onions and sauté for 10 to 12 minutes or until lightly browned. When the liver is cooked and still warm, cut into 2-inch chunks and place in a food processor with the steel cutting blade attachment. Process until the liver is well chopped, about 15 to 20 seconds. Place the chopped liver in a large bowl. Repeat the chopping process with the eggs, then the onions, adding each to the liver. Add the remaining ingredients and mix well again. Serve immediately or cover and chill until ready to use. Serve at room temperature.

NOTE: A super spread on crackers or served with lettuce and tomatoes.

# Smoked Salmon Dip

*I cup*

*Here's a I-2-3 throw-together dip that hails from Norway. Sure, my way has some shortcuts, but it still has the same great Scandinavian taste.*

½ cup (3 ounces) chopped smoked salmon
3 ounces cream cheese, softened
½ cup heavy cream
1 teaspoon lemon juice
½ teaspoon dried dill or
1½ teaspoons fresh dillweed, chopped
⅛ teaspoon white pepper

Combine all the ingredients in a large bowl. Using a hand mixer, blend with on and off strokes until the mixture is workable, then blend on low speed until the mixture is smooth and well mixed. Cover and chill until ready to use. Serve chilled or at room temperature.

NOTE: You can add a small seeded and finely chopped cucumber for a slightly different taste. Or you might want to cover the dip with chopped fresh parsley or pimiento. Serve it with rye or pumpernickel bread or your favorite crackers.

# Mediterranean Spinach Rolls

*16 pieces*

*The perfect nibble before dinner, or maybe for a snack all by itself—'cause the only thing you'll crave to go with these tastes of the Mediterranean is a cruise around the Greek islands!*

2 packages (10 ounces each) frozen spinach,
thawed and drained
½ envelope (from a 2-ounce box) onion soup mix
½ cup (2 ounces) crumbled feta cheese
2 eggs, each slightly beaten in its own dish
1 frozen puff pastry sheet (from a 17¼-ounce package),
slightly thawed

Preheat the oven to 350°F. Place the drained spinach in a medium-sized bowl. Add the onion soup mix, feta cheese, and 1 egg; mix well. On a lightly floured surface, with a rolling pin, roll out the puff pastry sheet into a 10" × 12" rectangle. Cut in half lengthwise and spread half the spinach mixture lengthwise along the center of each dough half. Using a pastry brush or paper towel, moisten the edges of the pastry dough with some of the remaining beaten egg. Evenly fold the dough lengthwise over the spinach. Seal the edges of the dough tightly by pressing the seams together with the tines of a fork. Brush the tops of both spinach rolls with beaten egg. Place on a cookie sheet and bake for 20 to 25 minutes or until the dough is puffed and golden brown. Cool slightly before cutting into 1½-inch slices.

NOTE: Make sure to bake these until the dough is golden brown because if they're underbaked, the pastry won't be nice and flaky.

# Hungarian Cheese Dip

*1 cup*

*Hungry? If you're peeking in here then I bet you are . . . and when you sample this cheese dip from Hungary, you'll be treating yourself to a traditional Old World specialty.*

1 package (8 ounces) cream cheese, softened
½ cup (1 stick) butter, softened
1 tablespoon paprika
1½ teaspoons caraway seeds
½ cup blue cheese dressing

In a medium-sized bowl, combine all the ingredients. Blend until smooth. Serve immediately or cover and chill until ready to use.

NOTE: Serve this with your favorite crackers, flat bread, or pitas.

# Wrapped-Up Brie

PARIS
C'EST SI BON!!
FRANCE

*3 to 4 servings*

*Brie is fancy, right? Your guests sure will be impressed, and with only two ingredients, you'll have more time to visit with them instead of staying in the kitchen cooking for them!*

1 frozen puff pastry sheet (from a 17¼-ounce package),
slightly thawed
2 brie cheese rounds (4½ ounces each), well chilled

Preheat the oven to 350°F. Roll out the puff pastry sheet on a lightly floured surface into a 10" × 12" rectangle. Cut the dough in half, making two 6" × 10" pieces, and place one brie round in the center of each half. Bring the ends up to the center, wrapping the dough around the cheese, and pinch the dough firmly to seal; cut off and discard any excess dough, being careful not to expose any brie. Place the bundles pinched end down on a cookie sheet that has been coated with nonstick vegetable spray. Bake for 25 to 30 minutes or until golden brown. Let cool slightly before cutting into small wedges.

NOTE: This can be eaten plain, but I like to add a fruity flavor by topping each bundle with a tablespoon of raspberry jam right after it comes out of the oven.

# Middle Eastern Dip

*4 cups*

*This is traditionally called hummus, and I can tell you that the first time I tasted it, I couldn't stop eating it! Now I serve it to my friends all the time and they can't stop eating it, either!*

2 cans (15 to 19 ounces each) garbanzo beans (chick peas),
drained and ⅓ cup of liquid reserved
3 garlic cloves, minced
¼ cup fresh lemon juice (juice of 2 to 3 lemons)
3 tablespoons olive oil
1½ teaspoons salt
1 teaspoon ground cumin

Combine all the ingredients in a food processor. Process until the mixture is smooth and creamy and no lumps remain, scraping down the sides of the bowl as needed. Serve immediately or cover and refrigerate until ready to use.

NOTE: Serve with pita bread triangles. If your pitas are a bit dry, try brushing them with a bit of olive oil and heating them in a warm oven for 5 minutes just before serving.

# Homestyle Soups

# Northern Ireland Potato Soup

*4 to 6 servings*

*The farmlands of Ireland always were perfect for growing potatoes—lots of potatoes. Now it takes us no time to cook up a pot of hearty potato soup just like the Irish served in their farmhouses of yesterday...*

2 cans (14½ ounces each) chicken broth
2 tablespoons (¼ stick) butter
2 celery stalks, chopped (½ cup)
4 medium-sized potatoes, diced (4 cups)
4 scallions, chopped (1 cup)
¼ teaspoon white pepper
1 tablespoon cornstarch
1 tablespoon water
1 pint heavy cream

In a soup pot, over medium-high heat, combine the chicken broth, butter, celery, potatoes, scallions, and pepper. Bring to a boil, then reduce the heat to low and simmer for 20 minutes, or until the potatoes are tender. In a small bowl, dissolve the cornstarch in the water, then slowly stir mixture into the soup, stirring constantly. Continue to simmer for 10 minutes more, stirring occasionally. Slowly stir in the heavy cream, stirring constantly until well mixed. Simmer for 5 more minutes and serve.

NOTE: Do not bring the soup to a high boil once you add the cream; that could cause the soup to curdle.

# Chicken in a Pot

*3 to 4 servings*

*Our ancestors used to let this cook all day long. Know what they got? A really tasty all-in-one meal. Now, with a few shortcuts, we can have almost the same taste in no time!*

2 cans (14½ ounces each) chicken broth
1 can (5 ounces) chunked breast of chicken, drained
1 can (14½ ounces) sliced carrots, drained
1 teaspoon onion powder
2 cups cooked medium egg noodles (4 ounces uncooked)

In a medium-sized saucepan, combine the chicken broth, chicken chunks, sliced carrots, and onion powder; bring to a boil over medium-high heat. Reduce the heat to low, add the cooked noodles, and cook for an additional 10 minutes to allow the tastes to "marry."

NOTE: If you have a bit of leftover chicken, remove the skin, pull it off the bone, and add it to the soup in place of the canned chicken. It'll make your soup extra-hearty.

# Chinatown Hot 'N' Sour Soup

*5 to 6 servings*

*I'm lucky that a friend shared his family's special soup recipe with me. It's been passed down from generation to generation. I made it even easier and now I get to pass it on to you. Aren't you glad we're family?!*

2 tablespoons cornstarch
1¼ cups water, divided
2 cans (10½ ounces each) condensed chicken broth
1½ cups (½ pound) firm tofu, cut into small chunks
¼ pound mushrooms, shredded or sliced to yield 2 cups
2 tablespoons white vinegar
1 teaspoon sesame oil
3 tablespoons Worcestershire sauce
2 tablespoons soy sauce
1 tablespoon ground ginger
1 teaspoon pepper
1 egg, lightly beaten

In a small bowl, mix the cornstarch and ¼ cup water into a paste; set aside. In a medium-sized saucepan, combine the 1 cup water, chicken broth, tofu, mushrooms, vinegar, sesame oil, Worcestershire sauce, soy sauce, ginger, and pepper. Bring the mixture to a boil over high heat. Reduce the heat to low, then slowly stir in the cornstarch mixture until soup thickens. Slowly stir in the beaten egg and simmer for 5 to 10 minutes, stirring occasionally.

NOTE: The pepper and ginger make this soup a bit spicy, so if you want it a bit milder, simply reduce the amount of each.

# Hungarian Goulash Soup

*4 servings*

*Here's a hearty Old World soup that's almost a meal by itself. With a loaf of dark rye bread and a green salad, you're all set!*

2 tablespoons (¼ stick) butter
1 medium-sized onion, chopped (about 1 cup)
1 pound ground beef
1 can (14½ ounces) crushed tomatoes
1 can (10½ ounces) condensed beef broth
½ cup water
1 can (15 ounces) potatoes, drained and cut into bite-sized pieces
2 teaspoons paprika
½ teaspoon salt

In a large saucepan, melt the butter over medium-high heat. Add the onion and sauté for 4 to 5 minutes, until golden brown. Add the ground beef and cook for 6 to 7 minutes, until browned, stirring occasionally. Stir in the remaining ingredients. Bring to a boil, then reduce the heat to low and simmer, uncovered, for 15 minutes.

NOTE: You guessed it—you could easily replace the ground beef with ground turkey or chicken . . . it's your choice!

# Mexican Black Bean Soup

*5 servings*

*Of course, you've heard of Mexican jumping beans! Well, this traditional soup uses black beans, and I'm sure everybody will jump up to the table when you serve this.*

2 cans (14 ounces each) black beans
2 cups water
1 jar (16 ounces) salsa
1 can (14½ ounces) vegetable broth
1 can (15¼ ounces) whole kernel corn, drained
2 teaspoons ground cumin

Combine all the ingredients in a large saucepan; bring to a boil over high heat. Reduce the heat to low and simmer for 15 minutes.

NOTE: Let me share a secret with you: If you don't have black beans, don't be afraid to use cannellini beans or red kidney beans. The soup will come out just as tasty.

# Simple Escarole Soup

*4 to 6 servings*

*Think chicken soup is the only soup that cures? Uh uh! This great old Italian soup is a cure, too—it's one of the tastiest cures for hungry appetites!*

3 cans (14½ ounces each) chicken broth
½ pound ground beef
2 tablespoons grated Parmesan cheese
¼ teaspoon garlic powder
¼ teaspoon salt
⅛ teaspoon pepper
1 small head escarole or ½ a medium-sized head,
coarsely chopped

Place the chicken broth in a large saucepan and heat over medium-high heat. Meanwhile, in a small bowl, combine the ground beef, Parmesan cheese, garlic powder, salt, and pepper. Roll the beef mixture into teaspoon-sized meatballs. Place the meatballs in the broth and bring to a boil. Reduce the heat to low and simmer for 10 to 12 minutes, or until the meatballs are cooked through. Add the escarole and cook for 5 to 7 more minutes.

NOTE: This can be served with cooked rice and topped with extra Parmesan cheese, if desired. You can even substitute fresh spinach for the escarole, if that's what you've got available. And when you make it with spinach, it'll be ready in 3 to 4 minutes, instead of 5 to 7.

# Beefy Russian Borscht

*4 to 5 servings*

*You can't get more authentic Old World than this, since I got the recipe from neighbors who made it often in their native Russia. I'm thankful to them for sharing!*

2 tablespoons olive oil
3 garlic cloves, minced
1 small onion, finely chopped (about ¾ cup)
½ pound stew beef or flank steak, cut into ½-inch chunks
2 cans (15 ounces each) julienned beets, undrained
1 can (8 ounces) tomato sauce
1 cup water
2 beef bouillon cubes
2 tablespoons sugar
1½ teaspoons lemon juice
1½ teaspoons salt

In a medium-sized saucepan, heat the oil over medium-high heat. Add the garlic, onion, and beef chunks, and sauté until the onion is tender and the meat is lightly browned. Add the remaining ingredients and bring to a boil. Reduce the heat to low and simmer for 35 to 40 minutes, stirring occasionally.

NOTE: Serve hot, and with the addition of a peeled boiled potato, you can have a hearty all-in-one meal.

# Worth-the-Wait Cabbage Soup

*12 to 16 servings*

*I got this recipe from my grandmother—and I know she got it from her mother. The original version had to be simmered for hours on her wood-burning stove. Boy, oh boy, I bet Great-Grandma would have loved our gas and electric ones!*

2 cans (28 ounces each) crushed tomatoes
1 can (12 ounces) tomato paste
Juice of 1 lemon
4 beef bouillon cubes
8 cups water
1 cup granulated sugar
½ cup firmly packed brown sugar
8 cups coarsely chopped green cabbage (1½ to 2 pounds)

In a soup pot, combine all the ingredients and heat over medium-high heat. Bring to a boil, then reduce the heat to low and simmer for 1½ to 2 hours.

NOTE: Since this recipe is meant to feed a crowd, don't be afraid to cut it in half or, even better, make all of it and freeze whatever's left over. It's just as good thawed and reheated.

# Hearty Minestrone Soup

*10 to 12 servings*

Sure, you can buy minestrone soup in a can, but why not try it this way for a change? You'll love the hearty Old World taste. And with a loaf of crusty Italian bread, you've got a satisfying meal.

3 cans (14½ ounces each) beef broth
1 can (15 ounces) red kidney beans
1 can (14 to 16 ounces) cannellini beans (white kidney beans)
1 can (28 ounces) crushed tomatoes
1 package (10 ounces) frozen chopped spinach
1 small onion, chopped (about ½ cup)
1 package (10 ounces) frozen mixed vegetables
1 teaspoon garlic powder
1 teaspoon salt
½ teaspoon pepper
1 cup uncooked elbow macaroni

In a soup pot, combine all the ingredients except the macaroni. Bring to a boil and add the macaroni. Reduce the heat to low and simmer for 30 minutes or until the macaroni is cooked.

NOTE: The true Italian way to serve it is topped with grated Parmesan cheese. Mmm!

ROME
AH
É MOLTO
BENE!!
ITALY

# "Try Sum" Egg Drop Soup

*6 to 8 servings*

*This is a Chinese restaurant favorite. Wonder how they do it? Here's how ... and it takes just a few minutes!*

4 cans (14½ ounces each) chicken broth, divided
1 teaspoon sesame oil
2 tablespoons cornstarch
2 eggs, beaten
½ cup thin angle-sliced scallions (1 to 2 scallions)
2 tablespoons soy sauce

In a large saucepan, over medium-high heat, bring 3½ cans of broth to a boil. Stir in the sesame oil and reduce the heat to low. In a small bowl, combine the cornstarch and the remaining ½ can of broth. Add to the soup, stirring constantly. With a fork, slowly stir the beaten egg into the soup, forming egg strands. Stir in the scallions and soy sauce and remove from the heat. Serve immediately.

NOTE: For a change, you may want to use only the whites of the eggs. Sure, that's okay, too.

BEIJING
啊! 很好吃!
CHINA

# Fast French Onion Soup

*6 to 8 servings*

*Oui, oui! It sure is quick and easy to make this soup, and the taste is just like what you'd enjoy at a French sidewalk café.*

2 tablespoons vegetable oil
2 medium-sized onions, cut into ¼-inch-thick slices
3 cans (14½ ounces each) beef broth
2 cups water
¼ teaspoon pepper
⅓ cup dry red wine
¼ cup grated Parmesan cheese

In a large saucepan, heat the oil over medium-high heat. Sauté the onions for 10 to 15 minutes, until browned. Stir in the beef broth, water, and pepper. Reduce the heat to low and simmer for about 20 minutes. Stir in the wine and cheese and continue cooking over low heat until mixed through. Serve immediately or keep warm until ready to use.

NOTE: Top with a few croutons and some shredded Swiss cheese. Watch—your gang won't be able to say anything but "Ooh, la la!"

# Portuguese Sausage Soup

*12 to 16 servings*

*Old-fashioned? Yes. Easy? Yes. Tongue-tingling taste? You guessed it . . . yes, yes, yes!*

1 medium-sized onion, diced (about 1 cup)
1 garlic clove, minced
1 can (28 ounces) crushed tomatoes
3 medium-sized carrots, chopped (1 cup)
½ a medium-sized head of cabbage, coarsely chopped
(about 4 cups)
3 cans (10½ ounces each) condensed beef broth
4 cups water
12 ounces chorizo sausage, casings removed and meat chopped
¼ teaspoon cayenne pepper
1 teaspoon salt
1 can (15 ounces) red kidney beans

In a soup pot, combine all the ingredients over medium-high heat; bring to a boil, then reduce the heat to low. Cover and simmer for 1 to 2 hours.

NOTE: The soup will be done after about an hour, but the longer you simmer it the heartier it will be. Chorizo is a specialty sausage that can be found in the refrigerated meat case of the supermarket. In case you want to substitute, you can use kielbasa instead.

# Spanish Garlic Soup

*4 to 5 servings*

*I almost called this "Garlic Lovers' Soup." Well, it is for garlic lovers, but I wanted to give credit to the early Spanish settlers.*

2 tablespoons olive oil
4 or 5 garlic cloves, minced
1 quart (4 cups) chicken broth or stock
¼ teaspoon salt
¼ teaspoon pepper
1 cup stale bread cubes (about 2 slices)
1 egg, beaten

In a soup pot, heat the olive oil over medium-high heat; sauté the garlic until golden. Remove the pot from the heat and cool slightly. Then return the pot to low heat and slowly add the stock, salt, pepper, and bread cubes; simmer for 2 to 3 minutes. Remove 2 tablespoons of the soup to a small bowl and mix with the beaten egg. Add the egg mixture back to the soup and stir. Continue cooking until the soup starts to thicken, about 2 minutes. Serve immediately.

NOTE: If you don't have any stale bread, this works just as well with croutons or toast cubes.

# Chilled Beet Borscht

*8 to 10 servings*

*Borscht was a staple of yesteryear throughout much of Eastern Europe because beets were so abundant (and so inexpensive!). I think it's making a comeback today, since more and more people are finding out how refreshing this cold vegetarian soup is!*

3 cans (15 ounces each) julienned, cut, or sliced beets, undrained
3½ cups water
¼ cup white vinegar
½ cup sugar
⅓ cup lemon juice
2 teaspoons salt
1 medium-sized cucumber, peeled and chopped
1 small onion, chopped (about ½ cup)
¾ cup sour cream
1¾ to 2 pounds potatoes, peeled and boiled

Place the beet juice in a soup pot. If using julienned beets, place them in the pot also. If using cut or sliced beets, place them in a large bowl and use a hand chopper to coarsely chop them. Add the chopped beets to the pot of beet juice and add the water, vinegar, sugar, lemon juice, and salt. Bring to a boil over medium-high heat, mixing occasionally. Remove from the heat and chill well before serving. Serve each bowl with 2 tablespoons chopped cucumber, 1 tablespoon chopped onion, 2 tablespoons sour cream, and ½ a boiled potato.

# Salad Accents

# Greek Island Salad

*4 to 6 servings (1 cup dressing)*

*The Coliseum, the aqueducts, and Greek Island Salad—three Old World classics.*

1 medium-sized head iceberg lettuce, cut into 1-inch chunks
1 medium-sized cucumber, peeled and diced (1½ cups)
¾ cup (about 4 ounces) feta cheese, crumbled
2 medium-sized tomatoes, cut into quarters
1 can (6 ounces) pitted large black olives or Greek-style olives,
drained

### DRESSING
¾ cup olive oil
⅓ cup lemon juice
1 tablespoon dried oregano
½ teaspoon garlic powder
½ teaspoon salt
¼ teaspoon pepper

Place the chopped lettuce on a platter. Top with the diced cucumber, then sprinkle with the feta cheese. Arrange the tomatoes on the cheese, then top the salad with the olives. In a small bowl, combine the dressing ingredients; mix well. Pour over the salad and serve.

NOTE: Greek-style olives are found at the supermarket deli counter or in the ethnic foods section.

# Little Italy Antipasto

*4 to 6 servings (1 cup dressing)*

*In an Italian meal, an antipasto course is traditionally eaten before the pasta course. With its combination of greens, meat, cheese, and marinated vegetables, this is a light salad that my family likes to make into a whole meal.*

1 medium-sized head iceberg lettuce, cut into bite-sized pieces
¼ pound thinly sliced ham
¼ pound thinly sliced Genoa or other hard salami
½ pound mozzarella cheese, cut into 1-inch chunks
2 medium-sized tomatoes, cut into chunks (about 2 cups)
1 jar (6 ounces) marinated artichoke hearts, drained
1 jar (7 ounces) roasted peppers, drained
¾ cup pepperoncini, drained
1½ cups extra-large pitted black olives (about 20), drained

DRESSING
½ cup olive oil
½ cup red wine vinegar
¾ teaspoon salt
¼ teaspoon white pepper

Place the lettuce on a large platter. Layer the remaining salad ingredients on top of the lettuce. In a small bowl, combine the dressing ingredients; mix well. Pour half of the dressing over the salad and add more as needed.

NOTE: Be creative when you do the layering of ingredients! An antipasto salad should always be colorful. I showed one on the

cover of this book to give you some ideas for making a really colorful salad for your gang. You can even add drained and flaked tuna, marinated mushrooms, etc. Add as much dressing as you like. There should be plenty of it, so if you like your salad drenched in dressing . . . go ahead and enjoy!

# Japanese Ginger Salad

*6 to 8 serving ( 1 ½ cups dressing)*

*With the popularity of Japanese restaurants, it's no wonder that I've gotten so many requests for a simple Japanese salad recipe that can be made at home. Here it is!*

### DRESSING
½ cup peanut oil
¼ cup white vinegar
¼ cup water
1 small onion, chopped (about ½ cup)
2 tablespoons soy sauce
2 tablespoons ketchup
2 teaspoons lemon juice
2 teaspoons sugar
2 teaspoons ground ginger
½ teaspoon salt
½ teaspoon pepper

1 head iceberg lettuce, coarsely chopped
2 medium-sized tomatoes, diced

Combine the dressing ingredients in a blender jar or food processor and blend until smooth. Just before serving, place the lettuce and tomatoes in a large bowl and toss with the dressing.

NOTE: If making this in advance, then make the dressing as above, cover, and chill. Toss with the lettuce and tomatoes just before serving.

# Israeli Chopped Salad

*6 to 8 servings (½ cup dressing)*

*Every culture has its own version of vegetable salads, and this Israeli salad is typical of how many Middle Eastern people prepare their salad vegetables. (Salad is so easy to eat when it's made this way!)*

2 medium-sized cucumbers, peeled, seeded, and diced (2 cups)
2 medium-sized green bell peppers, cored and diced (1½ cups)
3 medium-sized tomatoes, seeded and diced (1½ cups)
¼ cup chopped onion
1 can (2¼ ounces) sliced black olives, drained (½ cup)
1 can (15 to 19 ounces) garbanzo beans (chick peas), rinsed and drained

### DRESSING
⅓ cup olive oil
3 tablespoons lemon juice
½ teaspoon white pepper
1½ teaspoons salt
4 teaspoons white vinegar

In a large bowl, combine the cucumbers, green peppers, tomatoes, onion, olives, and garbanzo beans. In a small bowl, combine the dressing ingredients; mix well. Pour the dressing over the vegetables and stir to coat. Cover and chill for 2 to 3 hours or overnight, allowing the mixture to marinate before serving.

NOTE: If you can, make this a day in advance so that the flavors have more time to "marry."

# Creamy Polish Salad

*4 to 6 servings*

*Our Polish ancestors used the vegetables from their harvests to make fresh garden salads, and with the addition of a little sour cream, they made this creamy dish that has been passed down over the years.*

2 medium-sized cucumbers, peeled and thinly sliced (2 cups)
8 to 10 radishes, thinly sliced (1½ cups)
1 cup sour cream
2 tablespoons dried dill
½ teaspoon salt

Place the cucumbers and radishes in a large bowl. Add the remaining ingredients and toss until the vegetables are coated thoroughly.

NOTE: A dash or two of ground white pepper will add a real zing to this salad!

# Romanian Mushrooms

*4 to 6 servings*

*My grandmother's best friend usually had some of these in her icebox when I visited. So every time I taste them, I know I'm enjoying a taste of her Old Country.*

½ cup Italian dressing
1 teaspoon coarse-ground or Dijon-style mustard
½ teaspoon salt
¼ teaspoon pepper
1 pound fresh mushrooms, cleaned and patted dry

Combine all the ingredients except the mushrooms in a large bowl; mix well. Add the mushrooms and stir gently to coat well. Cover and chill for 3 to 4 hours or overnight, tossing occasionally.

NOTE: You can use prepared yellow mustard in place of the Dijon-style mustard for a more New World taste! If you happen to have some very large mushrooms, I suggest cutting those in half before adding them to the dressing mixture.

# Indian Refresher Salad

*8 to 10 servings*

*Indian food is known for its unique spices. Some of them are really hot, so to cool down the flavorings a bit, this traditional cucumber relish, called* raita, *is often served. It's usually made with grated cucumbers, but this way it's a bit easier—and still fresh and cooling.*

3 large cucumbers
1 small onion, grated (about ½ cup)
2 cups plain yogurt
½ teaspoon garlic powder
1 tablespoon dried mint leaves
¾ teaspoon salt
¼ teaspoon white pepper

Peel the cucumbers and slice in half lengthwise. Scoop out the seeds and coarsely chop the cucumbers. Place in a large bowl and add the remaining ingredients; mix well. Serve immediately or cover and chill until ready to use.

NOTE: When fresh mint is available, go ahead and use it. Coarsely chop 2 tablespoons fresh mint leaves and use in place of the dried mint.

INDIA
oh ye bahut
aeehaa hai!!
NEW DELHI

# British Pepper Salad

*4 to 6 servings*

*The English certainly have a winner with this salad!*

4 green bell peppers, cored and cut into 8 chunks
4 red bell peppers, cored and cut into 8 chunks
⅛ cup Worcestershire sauce
1¼ cups ketchup
1 can (6 ounces) pitted black olives, drained
1 garlic clove, crushed

Fill a 2-quart saucepan three-quarters full with water. Bring to a boil over medium heat. Add the peppers and stir gently once. After 2 to 3 minutes, when the peppers are still quite firm and just beginning to soften, remove them from the saucepan, draining any excess water. In a medium-sized bowl, combine the remaining ingredients. Add the peppers and toss to coat. Cover and chill for 1 hour or until ready to serve.

NOTE: This will keep in the refrigerator for up to 1 week, unless it's gobbled up before then!

# Mozzarella and Tomato Salad

*4 to 6 servings (¾ cup dressing)*

*You don't have to be Italian to love this fresh-tasting Old Country favorite.*

4 medium-sized tomatoes, cut into large chunks (about 4 cups)
1 pound mozzarella cheese, cut into 1-inch chunks

### DRESSING
½ cup olive oil
¼ cup balsamic vinegar
½ teaspoon dried basil
½ teaspoon salt
½ teaspoon pepper

Place the tomato and mozzarella chunks in a large bowl. Combine the dressing ingredients in a small bowl; mix well. Pour over the tomato and cheese mixture; toss to coat. Cover and chill for about 2 hours.

NOTE: Wanna get trendy? Use fresh mozzarella, also known as Buffalo mozzarella (it's available, usually packed in water, at the supermarket cheese counter) and top each serving with a sprig of fresh basil.

# Asian Cabbage Salad

*8 to 12 servings (2 cups dressing)*

*Our produce counters are now stocking a wider than ever selection of Asian vegetables, and Chinese cabbage is sure one of the most requested ones. When you toss some with this fast Asian-style dressing, you'll know why!*

## DRESSING
2 tablespoons peanut oil
½ cup sesame seeds
4 medium-sized garlic cloves, minced
2 tablespoons soy sauce
¼ cup white vinegar
½ cup sugar
¾ cup vegetable oil

1 head napa or Chinese cabbage, washed and cut into
bite-sized pieces

In a medium-sized saucepan, warm the peanut oil over medium heat. Sauté the sesame seeds and garlic for 3 to 5 minutes, until the seeds are golden brown. Reduce the heat to medium-low and add the soy sauce, vinegar, sugar, and vegetable oil; continue to cook for 2 more minutes. Place the cabbage in a large bowl and pour the desired amount of warm dressing over it, tossing to coat the cabbage evenly. Serve immediately.

NOTE: Refrigerate any remaining dressing for up to 1 month. Just reheat before adding to more cabbage.

# Tossed Green Beans and Tomatoes

*3 to 4 servings*

*Do you think that the fact that this salad is served chilled has anything to do with the fact that it comes from Chile?!*

2 packages (10 ounces each) frozen green beans,
thawed and drained
3 medium-sized tomatoes, coarsely chopped (about 3½ cups)
2 tablespoons olive oil
2 tablespoons fresh or bottled lemon juice
3 garlic cloves, finely minced
¾ teaspoon salt
¼ teaspoon hot pepper sauce

Place the green beans and the tomatoes in a large bowl. In a small bowl, combine the remaining ingredients, then pour over the green beans and tomatoes; mix well. Cover and chill for 3 to 4 hours or overnight, tossing occasionally.

NOTE: This is a perfect summer salad when the garden tomatoes are at their best and the green beans are fresh off the vine. If using fresh beans, all you have to do is steam them and allow them to cool before combining with the tomatoes, as directed above.

# Tuscany Bread Salad

*4 to 5 servings (³⁄₄ cup dressing)*

*In the Mediterranean this is called **panzanella**, which means "bread salad."
I know it sounds strange, but it's really good... and different. My shortcut
calls for store-bought croutons, so now it's a snap to toss together!*

### DRESSING
½ cup olive oil
¼ cup balsamic vinegar
½ teaspoon sugar
¼ teaspoon salt
¼ teaspoon pepper

1 pound ripe plum tomatoes, cut into wedges
¼ cup thinly sliced red onion
3 cucumbers (about 1½ pounds) peeled and thinly sliced
1 box (5½ ounces) croutons

In a small bowl, combine the olive oil, vinegar, sugar, salt, and
pepper; cover and set aside. In a large bowl, combine the remaining ingredients. Whisk the dressing and pour over the vegetables
and croutons. Toss and serve immediately.

NOTE: You can always get a different taste with this one by using
a different crouton flavor each time. Browse through the crouton
section next time you're in the supermarket.

# Fresh-from-the-Oven Breads

# Winning Yorkshire Pudding

*6 servings*

*If I had a favorite recipe in this chapter, this English-style popover would be it. Crispy outside and airy inside, it's the perfect roast beef go-along.*

2 cold eggs
1 cup cold milk
1 tablespoon butter, melted
1 cup all-purpose flour
½ teaspoon salt

Preheat the oven to 425°F. In a large bowl, combine all the ingredients, mixing with a wooden spoon until just blended (a few lumps may remain). Immediately pour into 6 muffin tins that have been coated with nonstick vegetable spray, filling each tin three-fourths full. Bake for 35 minutes or until golden brown and puffy.

NOTE: Serve these hot with butter or the pan drippings from your roast beef. They disappear really fast, so I suggest making a double batch!

OOH IT'S SO GOOD!!™ - LONDON
ENGLAND ENGLAND ENGLAND

# Baked French Toast

*6 to 8 servings*

*The Germans call this "nun's toast," the French call it "lost bread," and the viewer who shared it with me just calls it "incredible!!"*

4 tablespoons (½ stick) butter, divided
7 to 8 slices challah or other homestyle white bread, sliced
1 inch thick
1 can (11 ounces) mandarin oranges, drained
4 eggs
¼ cup milk
¼ cup sugar
1 teaspoon vanilla extract
½ teaspoon ground cinnamon
¼ teaspoon salt

Coat a 9" × 13" glass baking dish with nonstick vegetable spray. Melt 2 tablespoons of the butter on the bottom of the baking dish. Place the bread in the dish, squeezing slices to fit. In a food processor or blender, combine the mandarin oranges, eggs, milk, sugar, vanilla, cinnamon, and salt. Blend or process at medium speed until well blended; pour over the bread. Cover and refrigerate for 1 to 2 hours or until the liquid has completely soaked into the bread. Preheat the oven to 350°F. Melt the other 2 tablespoons of butter. Pour over the top of the bread. Bake for 1 hour, turning once halfway through cooking.

NOTE: Perfect for breakfast, brunch, or a dinner side dish—like a fruity stuffing, and it's a great way to use up day-old bread!

# Oven-Fresh Breadsticks

*10 sticks*

*Did you think that breadsticks just came in a package from the supermarket? They didn't always. And now, with my homemade-style shortcuts, you can have breadsticks hot from your oven to your table in no time!*

1 pound frozen bread dough, thawed
½ cup all-purpose flour
1 egg, beaten
¼ cup grated Parmesan cheese
3 teaspoons garlic powder
2 teaspoons sesame seeds

Preheat the oven to 350°F. Cut the thawed dough into ten ½-inch-thick slices. Lightly flour a cutting board and roll out each slice to about 12 inches long. Place the rolled dough on a cookie sheet that has been coated with nonstick vegetable spray. Brush each breadstick with the beaten egg. In a small bowl, combine the remaining ingredients and sprinkle on top of the dough. Bake for 15 to 20 minutes or until golden brown.

NOTE: Serve these hot from the oven. They're great for dipping in softened butter or even a rich spaghetti sauce.

MR. FOOD'S OLD WORLD

**OOH IT'S SO GOOD!!**™

COOKING MADE EASY

# Old-Fashioned Onion Board

*6 to 8 servings*

*My grandmother (we called her "Bubbie") used to talk about a flat bread that she always had as a kid—it was covered with lots of onions. Years ago, when I surprised her by making this quick version, she said it brought back lots of nice memories of her childhood in Europe.*

2 tablespoons (¼ stick) butter
1 medium-sized onion, minced (about 1 cup)
1 pound frozen bread dough, thawed
1 egg, beaten
½ teaspoon poppy seeds

Preheat the oven to 350°F. In a medium-sized skillet, melt the butter and cook the onion until soft. Roll out the bread dough and fit into a 10" × 15" rimmed cookie sheet. Brush with the beaten egg, then spread the cooked onion evenly over the top. Sprinkle with the poppy seeds and bake for 25 to 30 minutes.

# Pull-Apart Polish Babka

*8 to 10 servings*

*When we baked this in our test kitchen we had to make it again and again ... no, not because it didn't come out right, but because our staff kept eating it up!*

2 cans (17½ ounces each) refrigerated buttermilk biscuits
(8 biscuits per can)
⅓ cup sugar
1 teaspoon ground cinnamon
½ cup raisins

Preheat the oven to 350°F. Separate each biscuit dough into 8 biscuits. Cut each biscuit into 6 pieces and place the pieces into a large bowl. In a small bowl, combine the sugar, cinnamon, and raisins. Sprinkle the cinnamon mixture over the biscuit pieces and toss until evenly coated. Place the dough mixture into a Bundt pan that has been lightly coated with nonstick vegetable spray. Bake for 30 minutes. Let cool for 10 minutes, then invert the pan to release the babka ring.

NOTE: Because of the way this bakes, I like to pull apart the baked dough instead of cutting it. I know it sounds funny, but I think it tastes even better that way! Try it.

# My Way Bruschetta

*24 to 30 pieces*

Bruschetta *sure is fancy-sounding, but all it is is an Italian bread cut in half, topped with vegetables, cheese, and herbs, and baked. In my family's book, this is the easiest way to bring out the smiles.*

1 loaf (1 pound) Italian bread, cut in half lengthwise
1 garlic clove, minced
⅓ cup olive oil
¼ teaspoon salt
¼ teaspoon pepper
½ cup thinly sliced scallions
1 small tomato, chopped
1½ cups (6 ounces) shredded mozzarella cheese

Preheat the oven to 500°F. Place the bread cut side up on a foil-lined baking sheet; set aside. In a small bowl, combine the garlic, olive oil, salt, and pepper. Drizzle the mixture over the cut side of the bread. Sprinkle the bread with the scallions and tomato, then top with the cheese. Bake in the upper half of the oven for 5 to 7 minutes, or until the cheese melts and the edges of the bread turn brown. Cut into 1-inch pieces and serve as is, or try some of the options listed below.

NOTE: Instead of a loaf of Italian bread, you can use a couple of submarine rolls, if that's what you've got on hand. It'll be just as crunchy scrumptious. And you can try almost any other toppings and garnishes, like chopped sweet peppers, chopped fresh basil or other fresh herbs, sautéed sliced mushrooms and celery or olives and bell peppers, drained canned beans, or sliced pepperoni. Have fun, 'cause however you make it, it'll be your own special **"OOH IT'S SO GOOD!!™"**

# Irish Soda Bread

*6 to 8 servings*

*When I was growing up, I heard a rumor about leprechauns finding a pot of gold at the end of the rainbow. Have you heard that one, too? Maybe it wasn't gold after all, but Irish soda bread... well, it's as good as gold (as breads go, anyway)!*

4 cups all-purpose flour
½ cup (1 stick) butter, melted, plus 1 tablespoon for brushing top of bread
⅔ cup sugar
1 cup raisins
2 teaspoons baking powder
¼ teaspoon baking soda
⅛ teaspoon salt
2 eggs, beaten
2 cups buttermilk

Preheat the oven to 350°F. In a large bowl, combine all the ingredients except the 1 tablespoon butter; mix just until moistened. Place in a greased 9-inch round baking pan and bake for 1 hour or until a knife inserted in the center comes out clean. After removing from the oven, brush the top with the remaining melted butter.

NOTE: This is best served right from the oven, but you can rewarm it in a 200°F. oven for 10 minutes before serving, and, yes, I suggest brushing the top with a bit more butter at that time.

# Easy Herbed Onion Bread

*1 loaf*

*I wanted to include so many breads of yesterday in this book, but most of them were too much work. Not this one! "Easy" isn't just in the title—it's in the directions, too.*

1 large onion, finely chopped (about 1½ cups)
2 tablespoons (¼ stick) butter
3 cups biscuit baking mix
1 egg
1 cup milk
1 teaspoon dried basil
1 teaspoon dried dill

Preheat the oven to 350°F. In a large skillet, sauté the onion in the butter for 5 to 7 minutes or until tender. Meanwhile, combine all the remaining ingredients in a large bowl. Add the onion, mixing just until blended. Spoon into a greased 9" × 5" loaf pan. Bake for 55 to 60 minutes or until golden. Cool before removing from the pan.

NOTE: Freeze a loaf to have one on hand at all times. Just thaw it, warm it, and it tastes like fresh-baked.

SPAIN ¡AY QUÉ BUENO!

# Meats from Our Ancestors

# Saucy Pork Chops

*4 servings (3 cups sauce)*

*Wine, garlic, tomatoes, and capers are all important to northern Italian cooking. When we combine them with pork chops, we know why Italian chefs are known for their flavorings.*

2 tablespoons vegetable oil
4 medium-sized pork chops (6 to 7 ounces each)
1 can (14½ ounces) stewed tomatoes
½ cup dry white wine
2 medium-sized onions, sliced ¼ inch thick
1 tablespoon capers
1 teaspoon garlic powder
¼ teaspoon dried thyme leaves
½ teaspoon salt
¼ teaspoon pepper

In a large skillet, heat the oil over medium-high heat and add the pork chops. Brown the chops on both sides, about 2 to 3 minutes per side, then turn off the heat. In a large bowl, combine the remaining ingredients and mix well. Pour the mixture over the pork chops and cover. Simmer the pork chops over low heat for 15 to 20 minutes or until the chops are tender and no pink remains.

NOTE: Don't worry if you don't have any capers on hand or don't care for them—just leave them out. I wouldn't want you to miss out on this dish because of that!

# Sunday Leg of Lamb

*10 to 12 servings*

*Lamb is popular in so many regions of the world, from India to Greece, Italy, and France, the Middle East, and New Zealand. Now it sure can be popular at your table, since my way is so simple!*

3 tablespoons vegetable oil
1 teaspoon salt
½ teaspoon pepper
½ teaspoon ground thyme
½ teaspoon paprika
1 teaspoon garlic powder
1 teaspoon onion powder
1 bone-in leg of lamb (6 to 8 pounds)

Preheat the oven to 350°F. In a small bowl, combine all the ingredients except the lamb. Mix well, then, using a pastry brush or your hand, evenly coat all sides of the lamb. Place the lamb on a wire rack in a roasting pan. Bake for 2½ to 3 hours or until desired doneness.

NOTE: Carve the meat of the leg across the grain with a sharp knife and serve with the pan drippings or even Garden-Fresh Dipping Sauce (page 68).

# North and South American Casserole

*6 to 8 servings*

*This dish is a quick version of the South American hallacas, which is a cornmeal dough wrapped around a spicy meat mixture. My version combines the flavorful ideas of yesterday with the big Tex-Mex taste of today.*

1 package (8½ ounces) corn muffin mix
1¼ pounds ground pork or beef
1 medium-sized onion, chopped (about 1 cup)
1 medium-sized green bell pepper, chopped (¾ cup)
1 can (10¾ ounces) condensed tomato soup
1 teaspoon garlic powder
½ cup raisins

Preheat the oven to 350°F. In a medium-sized bowl, prepare the corn muffin mix according to the package directions, but do not bake; set aside the batter. In a large skillet, sauté the ground meat for 5 to 7 minutes or until crumbly. Remove the meat from the pan and drain well, reserving 2 tablespoons of the drippings in the pan. Sauté the onion and green pepper in the drippings over medium heat for 4 to 5 minutes or until soft. Return the drained meat to the pan and add the soup, garlic powder, and raisins; mix well. Pour the mixture into an 8-inch square baking dish that has been coated with nonstick vegetable spray. Spread the corn muffin mixture evenly over the meat mixture. Bake for 30 minutes or until the muffin topping is firm.

MR. FOOD®'S OLD WORLD

**OOH IT'S SO GOOD!!**™

COOKING MADE EASY

# European Stroganoff

*4 to 6 servings*

*Northern European stroganoff is traditionally made with chunks of beef. Today we can substitute ground beef and make an Old World favorite in just minutes.*

1 tablespoon butter
1 pound ground beef
1 medium-sized onion, chopped (1 cup)
1 can (8 ounces) mushroom stems and pieces, drained
2 tablespoons all-purpose flour
1 teaspoon garlic powder
½ teaspoon pepper
1 can (10½ ounces) cream of chicken soup
½ pound medium egg noodles
1 cup sour cream

In a large skillet, melt the butter over medium heat. Add the ground beef and onion and cook, stirring occasionally, until the meat is browned and the onion is tender. Add the mushrooms, flour, garlic powder, and pepper and cook for 5 minutes, stirring constantly. Reduce the heat to low and stir in the soup; simmer, uncovered, for 10 minutes, stirring occasionally. Meanwhile, cook the egg noodles according to the package directions; drain and place in a large bowl. Remove the meat mixture from the heat and stir in the sour cream. Spoon over the cooked noodles and serve.

# Old-Fashioned German Meatballs

*4 to 6 servings*

*Most people are familiar with Italian meatballs and Swedish meatballs. In case you haven't heard of German meatballs, please let me introduce you. Gee, maybe you'll want to make some of each for a meatball smorgasbord!*

1 pound ground beef
½ cup dry bread crumbs
1 teaspoon caraway seeds
1 teaspoon salt
½ teaspoon pepper
1 egg
1 bottle or can (12 ounces) beer
1½ cups ketchup

In a medium-sized bowl, combine the ground beef, bread crumbs, caraway seeds, salt, pepper, and egg; mix well. Form the mixture into 1-inch meatballs. In a medium-sized saucepan, combine the beer and ketchup and heat over medium-high heat. Add the meatballs and bring to a boil, then reduce the heat to low, cover, and simmer for 25 to 30 minutes.

NOTE: I like using a dark German beer 'cause it gives the sauce a really full taste, but any brand will work well. Why, you can even substitute ginger ale for the beer, if you prefer.

# Pick-a-Winner Picadillo

*3 to 4 servings*

*America isn't the only place where people love Sloppy Joes. Check out this Spanish dish that's a lot like ours, but with a little more pizzazz.*

2 tablespoons vegetable oil
1 pound ground beef
1 medium-sized onion, chopped (about 1 cup)
1 can (14½ ounces) whole peeled tomatoes, undrained,
broken up
½ cup chopped pimiento-stuffed olives
½ cup raisins
2 teaspoons chili powder
¼ teaspoon garlic powder
¼ teaspoon salt
¼ teaspoon pepper

SPAIN
¡AY, QUÉ BUENO!

In a large skillet, heat the oil over medium heat. Add the ground beef and onion and brown the beef until no pink remains. Add the remaining ingredients and mix well. Reduce the heat to low and simmer until the mixture is warmed through.

NOTE: I suggest serving this over rice. And you might want to add a bit of zing to your meal by adding a few drops of hot pepper sauce.

# Beef Bourguignon

*6 to 8 servings*

*Beef chuck is not one of the more tender meat cuts, but when it's simmered with lots of veggies, herbs, and wine in this classic French recipe, it comes out melt-in-your-mouth delicious!*

1 teaspoon dried thyme
1 teaspoon salt
1 teaspoon pepper
2½ pounds lean boneless beef chuck, cut into 1½-inch chunks
2 tablespoons vegetable oil
1 can (10½ ounces) beef broth
1 cup Burgundy or other dry red wine
2 garlic cloves, minced
½ pound carrots, peeled and cut into 1-inch chunks
½ pound potatoes, peeled and cut into 1-inch chunks
½ pound small whole fresh mushrooms, cleaned
1 package (10 ounces) frozen pearl onions
¼ cup water
2 tablespoons all-purpose flour

In a large bowl, combine the thyme, salt, and pepper. Add the beef pieces and toss to coat. In a large pot, heat the oil over medium heat; add half the beef and brown for about 10 minutes, stirring occasionally. Remove the beef to a bowl and pour off the drippings. Repeat with the remaining beef, then place the reserved beef back in the pot. Stir in the broth, wine, and garlic. Reduce the heat to low, cover tightly, and simmer for 1 hour, stirring occasionally. Add the carrots, potatoes, mushrooms, and onions; cover and continue cooking for another hour, stirring occasionally. In a small bowl, combine the water and flour; gradually stir the mixture into the stew. Continue cooking, uncovered, for about 10 more minutes or until slightly thickened, stirring occasionally.

NOTE: Don't be afraid to make a big batch, even if you need only a few servings, since this freezes well for other meals.

# Greek Lamb Kebabs

*30 to 35 medium-sized kebabs*

*These are like gyros on sticks, and when served with Garden-Fresh Dipping Sauce, it's all Greek to me!*

30 to 35 six- to eight-inch wooden or metal skewers
2½ to 3 pounds ground lamb
1 medium-sized onion, finely chopped (1 cup)
½ cup chopped fresh parsley
¼ cup tomato sauce
1 teaspoon salt
½ teaspoon pepper

If using wooden skewers, soak them in water for 15 to 20 minutes. Meanwhile, preheat the broiler to high. In a large bowl, combine all the ingredients; mix well. Roll the mixture into 30 to 35 sausage-like shapes 2 to 3 inches long and place on 2 broiler pans or rimmed cookie sheets. Place one skewer into the end of each lamb roll and broil for 5 to 7 minutes per side, turning once, until cooked through.

NOTE: You may want to cook these on the grill. That works, too! Just place the skewers across the grill rack of a preheated grill and cook as directed above.

*continued*

# Garden-Fresh Dipping Sauce

*3 cups*

1 cup plain yogurt
1 cup sour cream
1 large cucumber, peeled, and cut into chunks
4 garlic cloves
1½ teaspoons dried mint leaves
3 tablespoons olive oil
4 teaspoons red wine vinegar
½ teaspoon salt
½ teaspoon onion powder

In a food processor or blender, blend all the ingredients until smooth. Serve immediately or place in a medium-sized bowl, cover, and chill until ready to use.

# Shepherd's Pie

*6 to 8 servings*

*The English sure know how to make food quick and easy. It's a whole meal in one pan!*

1 pound lean ground beef
1 medium-sized onion, chopped (about 1 cup)
1 envelope (1.15 ounces) onion soup mix
1 can (10½ ounces) beef gravy
1 teaspoon garlic powder
½ teaspoon pepper
1 can (7 ounces) whole kernel corn, drained
1 can (16 ounces) sliced carrots, drained
1 package (10 ounces) frozen peas, thawed
5 cups warm seasoned mashed potatoes
(instant potatoes are fine)
Paprika for sprinkling

Preheat the oven to 350°F. In a large skillet, brown the ground beef and onion. Drain liquid, if necessary. Add the soup mix, gravy, garlic powder, and pepper; mix well. Add the corn, carrots, and peas. Place in a 2-quart casserole dish that has been coated with nonstick vegetable spray. Spread the mashed potatoes over the top and sprinkle with paprika. Bake for 25 minutes or until heated through. Allow to cool, then cover and store in the refrigerator until just before serving. Uncover and reheat at 350°F. for 25 to 30 minutes or in the microwave on high power until heated through. If planning more than 3 days ahead, wrap the pie well and freeze until the night before planning to serve. Let it thaw in the refrigerator overnight, then reheat as directed.

NOTE: If you'd rather have tomato sauce than gravy, try that instead. If you'd like, you can sprinkle ½ cup of your favorite cheese over the potatoes before sprinkling with paprika. And for even quicker preparation, you could use two 16-ounce bags of frozen mixed vegetables instead of the corn, carrots, and peas. The pie should be your own creation!

# Sicilian Meatball
# Sandwiches

*4 sandwiches*

*This recipe has assimilated into American tastes but it still says "Italy" in every bite.*

1 jar (26 ounces) spaghetti sauce, divided
½ cup fresh bread crumbs
1 small onion, finely chopped (½ cup)
¼ cup grated Parmesan or Romano cheese
1 egg
1 teaspoon dried parsley flakes
1 teaspoon garlic powder
1 pound ground beef
4 Italian sandwich rolls (each 6 inches long)

Preheat the oven to 350°F. In a large bowl, combine ⅓ cup of the spaghetti sauce, the bread crumbs, onion, cheese, egg, parsley, and garlic powder; mix well. Add the ground beef to the mixture and blend well. Shape into about sixteen 2-inch meatballs and arrange in a 9" × 13" baking pan. Bake for 20 minutes. Remove from the oven and drain the liquid. Pour the remaining sauce over the meatballs and return to the oven for 10 to 15 minutes more or until hot and fully cooked. Serve on the sandwich rolls.

# French Country One-Pot

*5 to 6 servings*

*I've seen recipes in lots of other cookbooks that are easy but use lots of pots and pans. Well, from the ingredients here you'll know you're in for a taste treat. And from the title, you'll know you're in for a cleanup treat, too!*

1 medium-sized onion, peeled, cut in half, and sliced
1 garlic clove, crushed
½ pound fresh Italian sausage
½ pound regular or reduced-fat fully cooked smoked sausage,
sliced diagonally into ½-inch slices
1 can (14 to 16 ounces) cannellini beans (white kidney beans)
rinsed and drained
1 can (15 to 19 ounces) garbanzo beans (chick peas), rinsed
and drained
1 can (14½ ounces) stewed tomatoes, undrained
2 tablespoons dry white wine (optional)
2 teaspoons brown sugar
1 teaspoon dried oregano
1 teaspoon dried thyme
Minced fresh parsley or sliced scallions for garnish (optional)

In a large saucepan that has been coated with nonstick vegetable spray, cook the onion and garlic over medium heat for 2 to 3 minutes, just until the onion is softened. Remove the Italian sausage from the casing and add to the saucepan. Cook and stir for 3 minutes. Add the sliced smoked sausage and cook for 3 to 5 minutes, or until the Italian sausage is cooked through and no pink remains. Pour off the drippings, then stir in the remaining ingredients except the parsley. Mix gently, then cover and reduce the heat to low. Simmer for 5 minutes, then uncover and cook over medium-low heat for 5 to 10 minutes to blend the flavors. Garnish with the parsley or scallions, if desired, and serve.

NOTE: Get out the rice or noodles to serve with this, 'cause the sauce is the best part.

# Mexican Steak

*3 to 4 servings*

*Years ago, the main cooking methods were over wood or coal stoves. Grilling is still popular, so that must mean that many of us enjoy that cooked-over-the-fire taste. And this South-of-the-Border recipe proves it.*

1 tablespoon chili powder
½ teaspoon ground cumin
½ teaspoon salt
¼ teaspoon cayenne pepper
1 boneless sirloin steak (2 to 2¼ pounds), 1½ to 2 inches thick 1 can (15 ounces) black beans, rinsed and drained
1 cup thick salsa (your favorite type)
Fresh cilantro sprigs for garnish (optional)

MR. FOOD®'S OLD WORLD
**OOH IT'S
SO GOOD!!**™
COOKING MADE EASY

In a small bowl or cup, combine the chili powder, cumin, salt, and pepper. Trim the fat from the steak and sprinkle the seasoning mixture over the steak, pressing it evenly into the entire surface (all sides) of the meat. Preheat the barbecue grill to medium heat and grill for 20 to 30 minutes for rare to medium meat, turning occasionally. Let stand for 10 minutes before carving. Meanwhile, in a medium-sized bowl, combine the beans and salsa; mix until blended. Slice the steak across the grain and arrange the slices on a serving platter. Top with the salsa mixture and garnish with cilantro sprigs, if desired.

NOTE: Use only as much of the seasoning mixture as you'd like; store any extra in an airtight container for future use (as long as it hasn't come in contact with the raw meat).

# Shortcut Moussaka

*6 to 8 servings*

*This is a traditional Turkish and Greek dish that typically has three or four layers of meat and eggplant with a custard topping. But I created a shortcut version that gives us the same Old World taste with half the work and half the cleanup!*

2 pounds ground beef
1 small eggplant, peeled and diced (about 4 cups)
3 garlic cloves, minced
⅛ teaspoon ground cinnamon
1½ teaspoons salt, divided
¼ teaspoon pepper
1½ cups spaghetti sauce
1 cup milk
2 eggs

Preheat the oven to 350°F. In a large skillet, sauté the ground beef over medium-high heat for 7 to 8 minutes, or until crumbly and only slightly pink; drain off any excess liquid. Add the eggplant to the skillet and sauté for 5 to 6 minutes, until the eggplant begins to soften. Add the garlic, cinnamon, 1 teaspoon of the salt, and the pepper; mix well. Add the spaghetti sauce and cook for 4 to 5 more minutes, until hot. Place the meat mixture in a 7" × 11" glass baking dish that has been coated with nonstick vegetable spray; smooth the top. In a small bowl, whisk together the milk, eggs, and remaining ½ teaspoon salt, then pour over the meat mixture. Bake for 40 to 45 minutes or until the custard-like top is set.

NOTE: If you want to make this a day or two before serving, go ahead. Just put it together up to the point of placing the meat mixture into the baking dish. Cover and refrigerate until ready to finish the dish, as directed above.

# Pizza Calzones

*8 servings*

*Many pizzerias make this popular northern Italian food. It's like a double-stuffed pizza, which makes it double yummy!*

½ pound bulk Italian sausage
2½ cups spaghetti sauce, divided
1 cup fresh mushrooms (2 to 3 ounces), sliced
1 small onion, chopped (½ cup)
½ cup chopped green bell pepper
1 teaspoon Italian seasoning
2 packages (8 ounces each) refrigerated crescent rolls (8 rolls per package)
1 cup (4 ounces) shredded mozzarella cheese
1 egg, beaten

Preheat the oven to 350°F. In a large nonstick skillet, brown the sausage for about 6 minutes over medium-high heat; drain any liquid and add ½ cup spaghetti sauce, mushrooms, onion, green pepper, and Italian seasoning. Simmer, uncovered, for 10 to 12 minutes. Meanwhile, unroll the crescent roll dough, separating each dough into 4 rectangles. Firmly press the perforations together on each rectangle and flatten slightly. Stir the cheese into the meat mixture and spoon about ¼ cup of the mixture onto half of each dough rectangle to within ½ inch of the edges. Brush the edges of the dough with some of the beaten egg and fold the dough over the filling, pressing to seal the edges. Arrange on a 10" × 15" rimmed cookie sheet and brush the tops with more of the beaten egg. Bake for 15 to 20 minutes, or until golden brown. Heat the remaining spaghetti sauce and serve with the calzones.

# Sweet-and-Sour Pork

*3 to 4 servings*

*Your gang will love this big Chinese taste, and you'll love how easy it is to impress them. Why not go a little further and have fortune cookies for dessert?*

2 tablespoons vegetable oil, divided
2½ to 3 pounds country-style pork ribs
3 medium-sized carrots, sliced (1 cup)
1 large green bell pepper, sliced into ¼-inch strips
1 can (20 ounces) pineapple chunks, drained and juice reserved
2 tablespoons soy sauce
3 tablespoons white vinegar
¼ cup firmly packed brown sugar
2 tablespoons water
1 tablespoon cornstarch

In a large skillet, heat 1 tablespoon of the oil over medium-high heat. Add the ribs and brown for 10 minutes; remove the ribs from the skillet and set aside. Add the remaining oil to the skillet and heat over medium-high heat. Add the carrots and green pepper and sauté for 3 to 5 minutes. Add the reserved pineapple juice, soy sauce, vinegar, and brown sugar, and cook over medium heat until hot. In a small bowl, combine the water and cornstarch and slowly add to the pineapple juice mixture. Bring the mixture to a boil, stirring occasionally, until thickened. Add the pineapple chunks and the ribs to the skillet. Cover and simmer over low heat for 20 to 25 minutes, until the meat is completely cooked and no pink remains.

NOTE: Country-style pork ribs are meatier than traditional pork ribs—which means more **"OOH IT'S SO GOOD!!™"**

# German-Style Stuffed Veal Cutlets

*6 to 8 servings*

*Shh! Listen! No, really...Do you hear the beat of an Oom-pah-pah band?
Or is that your family banging on the table 'cause they want more?!*

1 cup one-step stuffing mix
1 egg
½ cup beef broth (ready to use)
1¼ to 1½ pounds (6 to 8) veal cutlets, pounded to ⅛-inch
thickness
1 package (8 ounces) cooked breakfast sausage links, divided
(about 10 links per package)
¼ teaspoon salt
⅛ teaspoon pepper
1 can (10½ ounces) mushroom gravy
1 medium-sized tomato, cut into quarters
1 small onion, cut into quarters

Preheat the oven to 350°F. In a small bowl, combine the stuffing
mix, egg, and beef broth. Place about 2 tablespoons of the stuffing
mixture on each piece of veal. Place a sausage link over the stuffing mixture, then roll up the veal and secure each cutlet with a
toothpick. Place the veal rolls in a 7" × 11" baking pan that has
been coated with nonstick vegetable spray, then sprinkle with the
salt and pepper. In a food processor or blender, combine the gravy,
tomato, onion, and remaining sausage links and blend on high

speed until fairly smooth. Pour over the veal rolls. Bake, uncovered, for 40 to 45 minutes, or until the veal is cooked through. Remove the toothpicks before serving.

NOTE: These sure are great for company or for a special family dinner!

# Skillet Corned Beef and Cabbage

*4 to 6 servings*

*It happens once a year—you make corned beef and cabbage for St. Paddy's Day and you love it so much that you wonder why you don't make it more often. Think it takes too much time and work? Not this way . . . so go ahead and make it all during the year!*

2 tablespoons vegetable oil
8 cups shredded green cabbage (½ a large head)
½ teaspoon salt
¼ teaspoon pepper
2 cans (15 ounces each) whole potatoes, drained
1 can (14½ ounces) sliced carrots, drained
¾ pound deli-style corned beef, sliced into ½-inch strips

In a large skillet, heat the oil over medium heat. Add the cabbage and sauté for 6 to 8 minutes, until very soft but not brown. Add the salt and pepper; mix well. Add the potatoes, carrots, and corned beef; mix to distribute evenly. Reduce the heat to medium low, cover, and cook for 6 to 8 minutes or until completely heated through. Serve immediately.

NOTE: I like to rinse my canned potatoes and drain them well before using.

MR. FOOD'S OLD WORLD
**OOH IT'S SO GOOD!!**™
COOKING MADE EASY

# Melt-in-Your-Mouth Swiss Steak

*4 to 5 servings*

*Once you see how tender this steak is, you'll be yodeling for more!*

½ cup all-purpose flour
1¼ teaspoons salt, divided
½ teaspoon pepper, divided
2 pounds cubed steak
6 tablespoons vegetable oil, divided
¾ cup chopped celery (about 2 stalks)
1 small onion, chopped (about ½ cup)
1 can (14½ ounces) sliced carrots, drained
1 jar (28 ounces) spaghetti sauce

In a medium-sized bowl, combine the flour, 1 teaspoon salt, and ¼ teaspoon pepper; coat the steak with the mixture. In a large skillet, heat 4 tablespoons of the oil over medium-high heat; add the steak and cook for 6 to 8 minutes, turning halfway through. Remove the steak from the skillet and set aside. In the same skillet, heat the remaining 2 tablespoons of oil over medium-high heat and sauté the celery and onion for about 5 minutes or until tender. Add the carrot slices, spaghetti sauce, and the remaining salt and pepper; mix well. Add the steak to the mixture, reduce the heat to low, and simmer, uncovered, for 10 minutes or until warmed through.

NOTE: Oh, if your skillet is not large enough to cook all the steak at once, cook it in two batches, adding more oil if needed.

# All-in-One Kielbasa

*4 servings*

*Polish kielbasa is a wonderful gift brought from the Old Country, and when we make it with sauerkraut and bacon, we come up with the most hearty, authentic taste.*

5 slices fresh bacon, or 4 tablespoons bacon bits
1 bag (32 ounces) sauerkraut, drained (4 cups)
1 can (4 ounces) sliced mushrooms, drained
¼ teaspoon celery seed
1 pound kielbasa

In a large skillet, fry the bacon slices over medium-high heat for 6 to 8 minutes or until crispy. Remove from the skillet, allow to cool, and crumble into small pieces in a small bowl. Meanwhile, drain all but 1 tablespoon of fat from the skillet, then add the sauerkraut, mushrooms, and celery seed to the skillet; add the crumbled bacon and mix well. Reduce the heat to low and add the whole kielbasa and simmer, covered, for 10 minutes or until heated through.

NOTE: Serve this cut into chunks with spicy coarse-ground mustard and enjoy!

# Not-Rolled "Rolled" Cabbage

*8 servings*

*I grew up watching my mom spend hours making her big pots of rolled cabbage. Sure, they were delicious, but it was so much work for her to steam the cabbage, pull it apart, and roll the stuffing in it. I came up with a quick way that tastes just as good and takes much less effort.*

1¼ pounds ground beef
½ cup dry bread crumbs
1 egg
1 teaspoon salt
¼ teaspoon pepper
1 medium-sized head green cabbage, shredded (12 to 14 cups)
1 can (16 ounces) jellied or whole-berry cranberry sauce
1 jar (28 ounces) spaghetti sauce
1 tablespoon lemon juice
5 gingersnap cookies, crumbled (about ¼ cup crumbs)

In a medium-sized bowl, combine the ground beef, bread crumbs, egg, salt, and pepper. Form the mixture into 1-inch meatballs (about 1 tablespoon each). Place half the shredded cabbage in a large pot, then add the meatballs. Spread the cranberry sauce over the meatballs, then add the remaining cabbage. Pour the spaghetti sauce over the mixture and **do not stir**. Bring to a boil, then reduce the heat to low and simmer, uncovered, for 20 minutes. Stir gently, being careful not to break up the meatballs. Simmer for another 25 minutes. Add the lemon juice and cookie crumbs, mix well, and simmer for 15 more minutes.

NOTE: If you're one of the folks who likes this on the sweeter side, add a tablespoon or two of dark brown sugar.

# Complete Lamb Stew

*6 to 8 servings*

*Isn't it great? A whole meal cooked in one pot! I wonder if our ancestors knew how thankful we'd be to them for making our lives easier today.*

3 to 3¼ pounds boneless lamb stew meat
2 medium-sized onions, coarsely chopped (about 2 cups)
1 to 2 carrots, sliced (1 cup)
3 garlic cloves, minced
1 can (28 ounces) crushed tomatoes, drained
1 cup canned beef broth
1 teaspoon ground cinnamon
1 teaspoon salt
½ teaspoon pepper
1 package (9 ounces) frozen green beans, thawed and drained
1 cup uncooked long- or whole-grain rice

In a soup pot, sauté the lamb over medium-high heat until brown. Add the onions, carrot, garlic, tomatoes, broth, cinnamon, salt, and pepper. Bring to a boil, then reduce the heat to low and simmer, covered, for 40 to 50 minutes. Add the green beans and rice and simmer for 25 minutes, or until the rice is tender.

NOTE: You could use any cut of boneless lamb—just cut it into 1-inch cubes and cook away!

# Old-Standby Pot Roast

*5 to 6 servings*

*What could be better for Sunday dinner when the whole family gets together? And since it's got so much long-cooked flavor, it's the perfect way to turn a less-expensive beef cut into a tasty, tender meal.*

3 to 3½ pounds beef bottom round roast
1 medium-sized onion, chopped (1 cup)
1 to 2 carrots, sliced (1 cup)
½ cup dry red wine
½ cup water
1 tablespoon crushed garlic
1 tablespoon dried tarragon leaves
¼ teaspoon salt
¼ teaspoon pepper

Preheat the oven to 325°F. Place the roast in a baking pan. Combine the remaining ingredients in a medium-sized bowl and pour over the meat. Bake for 1½ to 2 hours or until the meat is fork-tender.

NOTE: Make sure you serve this with the pan drippings. They've got so much flavor!

# Spanish Country Lamb Chops

*4 servings*

*With a quick look at these ingredients, you might think, "Hmm, that's a strange combination." Well, I agree—but once you try the final dish, you'll know why this Spanish recipe is always a hit.*

1 tablespoon olive oil
4 lamb chops (about 8 ounces each)
1 can (10¾ ounces) condensed cream of celery soup
1 medium-sized tomato, chopped (about 1 cup)
1 teaspoon garlic powder
⅛ teaspoon dried thyme leaves
¼ pound pre-sliced pepperoni (about 1 cup)

SPAIN ¡AY ¡QUÉ BUENO!

In a large skillet, heat the olive oil over medium heat and brown the chops, about 6 minutes per side. Reduce the heat to low. In a medium-sized bowl, combine the remaining ingredients and mix well. Add the mixture to the skillet, covering the chops. Cover the skillet and simmer for 25 minutes or until tender. Remove the meat from the skillet and stir the sauce constantly for 1 to 2 minutes before removing from the heat and serving over the chops.

NOTE: You can use rib chops instead of shoulder, but simmer them for 10 minutes less (15 minutes total simmering time).

# Ukrainian Garlic-Crusted Liver

*4 to 6 servings*

*Just for fun, I had ten people taste this without knowing what it was. Nine times I heard, "I love it!" and then, "I can't believe it's liver!" That's because it was so moist and bursting with garlic flavor. (By the way, the tenth one knew it was liver and wouldn't give in . . . okay, nothing's perfect, but I try!)*

4 beef or calf's liver steaks (1½ to 2 pounds total)
¼ cup seasoned bread crumbs
4 large garlic cloves, finely chopped
¼ teaspoon pepper
¼ teaspoon salt
1 tablespoon dried parsley flakes
Nonstick vegetable spray

Preheat the oven to 400°F. Place the liver in a 9" × 13" baking dish that has been coated with nonstick vegetable spray. In a small bowl, combine the remaining ingredients and sprinkle over the steaks. Spray the steaks with vegetable spray and bake for 20 minutes or until desired doneness.

NOTE: Beef and calf's liver do not have to be cooked until they're dry and hard. Try cooking them to medium-well so that they're still moist and flavorful.

# Oniony Polish Sausage

*6 servings*

*I get lots of questions about how to make Polish kielbasa other than grilling it. Now I've got the answer for everybody.*

2 tablespoons vegetable oil
1 large onion, cut into ¼-inch slices (1½ cups)
1 can (10¾ ounces) condensed onion soup
1 tablespoon white vinegar
¼ teaspoon pepper
1 pound Polish kielbasa
1 can (14½ ounces) whole potatoes, drained
1 can (14½ ounces) sliced carrots, drained

In a large skillet, heat the oil over medium-high heat and cook the onion for about 5 minutes, until tender. Stir in the soup, vinegar, and pepper. Pierce the skin of the kielbasa several times with a fork, then add it along with the potatoes and carrots; reduce the heat to low, cover, and cook for 15 minutes or until heated through. Serve immediately.

NOTE: Piercing the kielbasa before heating helps keep it from bursting open while it's cooking.

# Dynasty Beef

*6 servings*

*The tastes of Asia with the ease of good old Sunday pot roast. Now, that's my kind of cooking!*

3 tablespoons soy sauce
3 tablespoons dry white wine
3 tablespoons sweet-and-sour or duck sauce
1 tablespoon red wine vinegar
1 teaspoon sugar
3 tablespoons peanut oil
1 teaspoon ground ginger
2 garlic cloves, chopped
¼ teaspoon crushed red pepper
One 3- to 3½-pound beef roast

Preheat the oven to 350°F. In a small bowl, combine all the ingredients except the beef and stir well. Place the beef in an 8-inch square baking dish and pour the sauce over the top. Cook, uncovered, for 1½ to 2 hours or to desired doneness, basting occasionally. Remove the meat from the oven and slice thinly across the grain. Serve with the pan drippings.

NOTE: To really enhance the flavor of the meat, let the roast marinate in the sauce for 2 to 3 hours or even overnight, turning it once halfway through so the whole roast gets the flavor.

# Osso Buco

*4 servings*

*No, Osso Buco isn't an Italian opera, but it is Italian. It's the traditional way of slow-cooking veal shanks with garlic, lemon, and parsley. Aha! Maybe you'll sing with delight, but it's still not an opera!*

¼ cup all-purpose flour
¼ teaspoon pepper
4 veal or lamb shanks (12 to 14 ounces each)
3 tablespoons vegetable oil
1 can (10¾ ounces) condensed onion soup
1 medium-sized tomato, chopped (about 1¼ cups)
1 cup dry white wine
½ cup plus 2 tablespoons water, divided
2 tablespoons lemon juice
1 tablespoon chopped fresh parsley
½ teaspoon garlic powder
3 tablespoons cornstarch
2 cans (14½ ounces each) whole potatoes, drained
1 can (14½ ounces) diced carrots, drained

In a shallow dish, combine the flour and pepper. Coat the shanks with the flour mixture. In a soup pot, heat the oil over medium-high heat and brown the shanks, about 5 minutes per side. Add the soup, tomato, wine, ½ cup water, lemon juice, parsley, and garlic powder; reduce the heat to low, cover, and simmer for 2 hours or until tender, stirring occasionally. In a small bowl, combine the cornstarch and 2 tablespoons water and stir into the pot until the liquid thickens. Add the potatoes and carrots and simmer for 10 to 15 minutes more until heated through.

NOTE: Osso Buco is normally served over cooked rice or pasta, but because this version has potatoes and carrots, you've got an easy one-pot meal.

# Mouth-Watering Pork Chops

*4 servings*

*Because we want to be sure our pork chops are completely cooked, we often cook them to the point of being tough and dry. I set out to update a European recipe that keeps them moist and saucy, and here's the result...*

¼ cup all-purpose flour
1 teaspoon salt
1 teaspoon pepper
4 thick pork chops (6 to 8 ounces each)
3 tablespoons butter
1 medium-sized ripe tomato, chopped (about 1¼ cups)
4 garlic cloves, chopped
2 cups sliced mushrooms
1 teaspoon browning and seasoning sauce
1 teaspoon minced fresh parsley
½ cup white wine or water

Place the flour, salt, and pepper in a shallow dish; mix well. Coat the chops with the flour mixture. In a large skillet, heat the butter over medium heat; add the chops and brown on both sides until golden, about 4 minutes per side. Remove the chops from the pan and set aside. Reduce the heat to low and add the remaining ingredients to the liquid in the skillet; stir well. Add the chops to the skillet, cover, and simmer for 20 minutes or until no pink remains in the center of the chops.

# Spicy Lamb-Stuffed Peppers

*8 servings*

*How 'bout a quick trip to the Middle Eastern desert? I'm thinking about a trip without the sand and the spitting camels . . . C'mon and make these spicy stuffed peppers as not just a side dish, but a center of the plate main course!*

8 medium-sized red, yellow, or green bell peppers
1½ pounds lean ground lamb
1 large onion, finely chopped (about 1¼ cups)
2 cups cooked rice
½ cup ketchup
½ cup raisins
1 teaspoon ground allspice
½ teaspoon ground cumin
½ teaspoon ground cinnamon
½ teaspoon black pepper
2 eggs, lightly beaten
1½ teaspoons salt
¼ teaspoon cayenne pepper

Preheat the oven to 375°F. Slice off the tops of the bell peppers and remove the seeds. Remove the stems and finely chop the cleaned pepper tops. Stand the peppers cut end up in a 9" × 13" baking dish that has been coated with nonstick vegetable spray. Brown the lamb in a large skillet over medium-high heat for 5 to 7 minutes, until no pink remains, stirring often to break up the meat; drain the liquid. Add the onion and chopped pepper. Cook, stirring, for about 5 minutes, until the onion is tender; remove from the heat. Stir in the rice, ketchup, raisins, allspice, cumin, cinnamon, black pepper, and eggs; blend well. Stir in the salt and cayenne pepper. Fill the peppers with the rice mixture, packing lightly. Cover with aluminum foil and bake for 40 to 50 minutes, or until the peppers are soft and can be pierced with a fork.

# Cuban Shredded Beef

*4 to 5 servings*

*When I was trying to decide what to order in a Cuban restaurant, I asked my waiter about this dish. It was called* ropa vieja, *which means "old shredded rags." He said it got its name because the beef cooks for so long that that's what it looks like. I loved the taste, but didn't want to have to wait two to three hours when I made it myself. You know I had to find a shortcut!*

3 tablespoons vegetable oil, divided
1¼ to 1½ pounds boneless stew beef
1 medium-sized yellow onion, chopped (about 1 cup)
1 medium-sized green bell pepper, chopped (about 1 cup)
2 garlic cloves, chopped
1 can (8 ounces) tomato sauce
1 teaspoon salt
1 teaspoon pepper
1 teaspoon chili powder

In a large skillet, heat 2 tablespoons of the oil over medium-high heat. Add the meat and brown; drain, remove to a bowl, and set aside to cool. When cool, use a food processor with a grating or cutting blade to process the beef until shredded. Add the remaining 1 tablespoon oil to the skillet and sauté the onion, green pepper, and garlic over medium-high heat for 4 to 5 minutes. Add the shredded beef and other remaining ingredients; cover, reduce the heat to low, and simmer for 10 to 15 minutes until the mixture is heated through.

NOTE: Create a great meal by serving this with cooked brown rice and some crusty bread.

# English Two-in-One

*6 to 8 servings*

*Yup, two favorites—Old Country sausage baked in a puffy Yorkshire pudding. Just scoop and enjoy!*

1 cup all-purpose flour
1 teaspoon salt
1 cup milk
¼ cup cold water
3 eggs, lightly beaten
1 pound mild rope sausage, cut into 1½- to 2-inch pieces

Preheat the oven to 450°F. In a medium-sized bowl, combine the flour and salt; add the milk a little at a time and beat with an electric mixer until smooth. Add the water and eggs and beat until bubbly. Cover loosely and set aside for ½ hour in a cool place, but do not refrigerate. Meanwhile, place the sausage in a 9" × 13" baking pan and bake for 20 minutes. Remove from the oven and pour the batter over the sausage. Bake on the center oven rack for 25 to 30 minutes or until puffy, well browned, and crisp.

NOTE: Spoon out the Yorkshire pudding and sausage so that you get two favorites in *every* mouthful!

# Tied-Up Breast of Veal

*6 to 8 servings*

*Too often we shy away from big cuts of meat like veal breast because we think it's too hard to cook. Well, here's the proof that it can be delicious and easy . . . and it won't tie you up in the kitchen all day!*

1 teaspoon onion powder
1 teaspoon garlic powder
1 teaspoon Italian seasoning
1 teaspoon salt
⅛ teaspoon pepper
1 tablespoon olive oil
One 3- to 4-pound boneless breast of veal, rolled and tied
(see Note)
1 can (14½ ounces) chicken broth
¾ cup water, divided
2 tablespoons all-purpose flour

Preheat the oven to 450°F. In a small bowl, combine the onion powder, garlic powder, Italian seasoning, salt, pepper, and olive oil; mix well. Rub the mixture over the veal, coating evenly. Pour the chicken broth into a 9" × 13" baking dish. Place the veal in the dish. Bake for 30 minutes, then reduce the heat to 350°F. and roast for an additional 50 to 60 minutes, or until desired doneness, basting occasionally. When the veal is finished roasting, remove it from the pan and add ¼ cup water to the drippings, making sure to loosen all the drippings. Transfer the liquid to a medium-sized saucepan and bring to a boil over medium-high heat. Meanwhile, in a small bowl, combine the remaining water and flour. Slowly add to the drippings, stirring constantly until thickened. Remove from the heat and serve over the sliced veal.

NOTE: If you ask, your butcher should be glad to roll and tie a boneless veal breast for you.

# Monte Carlo Brisket

*12 to 15 servings*

*Monte Carlo is known for its night life, gambling, and fine food. Well, this recipe is definitely fine, and in my opinion it's a sure winner... with no gamble!*

One 4- to 5-pound beef brisket
1 can (28 ounces) crushed tomatoes
1 envelope (from a 2-ounce box) onion soup mix
2 tablespoons balsamic vinegar
1 teaspoon dried oregano
1 teaspoon garlic powder
½ teaspoon pepper

Preheat the oven to 350°F. Place the brisket in a roasting pan that has been coated with nonstick vegetable spray. In a large bowl, combine the remaining ingredients. Pour over the brisket, cover tightly with aluminum foil, and bake for about 3 hours or until the meat is fork-tender. Slice the brisket across the grain and serve with the pan drippings.

NOTE: If you want to make this in advance, just put the sliced brisket back into the pan of drippings, cover, and keep refrigerated. Then heat it in the oven just before serving.

# Immigrant Short Ribs

*4 servings*

*These may take a while to cook, but they prove the old saying that "Good things come to those who wait."*

3 pounds beef short ribs
1 medium-sized onion, chopped (about 1 cup)
3½ cups water
3 tablespoons Worcestershire sauce
2 teaspoons paprika
2 teaspoons salt
¼ teaspoon pepper
2 large potatoes, peeled and cut into ½-inch slices
2 carrots, peeled and cut into 1-inch chunks
2 celery stalks, cut into 1-inch pieces
½ cup (3 ounces) raw medium barley

In a large pot, combine the short ribs, onion, water, Worcestershire sauce, paprika, salt, and pepper; bring to a boil. Reduce the heat to low, cover, and cook for about 1½ hours, stirring occasionally. Add the potatoes, carrots, celery, and barley; cook for an additional hour, stirring occasionally and adding more water, if necessary.

NOTE: This is one of those even-better-when-reheated-the-next-day recipes. Before reheating, be sure to remove any fat that has solidified on the top.

# "Luck of the Irish" Stew

*6 to 8 servings*

*Could I have an Old World cookbook without Irish stew? No way! It'd be like St. Patrick's Day without corned beef and cabbage.*

¼ cup all-purpose flour
1 teaspoon salt
1 pound boneless lamb, cut into 1-inch chunks
¼ cup vegetable oil
2 medium-sized onions, peeled and quartered
2 large carrots, peeled and cut into 1-inch slices
4 medium-sized potatoes (about 1½ pounds), peeled and cut into sixths
1 can (14½ ounces) beef broth
½ cup tomato sauce (½ an 8-ounce can)
¼ teaspoon ground thyme
1 teaspoon pepper

In a small bowl, combine the flour and salt. Add the lamb and coat completely. In a soup pot, heat the oil over medium-high heat. Add the lamb and any extra flour that is left in the bowl. Sauté for 4 to 5 minutes, until the lamb is lightly browned. Add the onions, carrots, and potatoes. Sauté for 1 minute, then add the beef broth, tomato sauce, thyme, and black pepper. Reduce the heat to low and simmer, stirring occasionally, for 45 minutes to 1 hour or until the lamb and potatoes are cooked through and tender.

# New Sauerbraten

*6 to 8 servings*

*Every sauerbraten recipe I came across called for two to four days of mar-*
*inating. Well, that may have been fine in the days of yesteryear, but we don't*
*usually want to wait that long! Here's an alternative that captures the flavors*
*of a true Old World favorite.*

3 tablespoons vegetable oil
2 tablespoons apple cider vinegar
1 can (12 ounces) ginger ale
⅓ cup lemon juice
2 tablespoons sugar
¾ teaspoon garlic powder
⅛ teaspoon ground cloves
½ teaspoon salt
¼ teaspoon pepper
2 bay leaves
1 small onion, chopped (about ½ cup)
One 2- to 2½-pound top round of beef (1½ inches thick)
1 tablespoon cornstarch

In a medium-sized bowl, combine all the ingredients except the beef
and cornstarch. Place the beef in a 7" × 11" glass baking dish.
Pour the mixture over the beef, cover, and refrigerate for 2 hours
or overnight, turning occasionally. Remove the meat from the marinade and place in a large skillet. Add the cornstarch to the marinade and mix well. Brown the meat over medium-high heat for 5

minutes per side. Reduce the heat to medium-low, add the corn-starch mixture, cover, and cook for 20 to 25 minutes or until de-sired doneness. Thinly slice the meat across the grain and serve with the pan juices. **Be sure to remove the bay leaves before serving**.

# Hot Tamale Pie

*4 to 5 servings*

*"Chili today, hot tamale!" Is it the weather report? No, but it can be you announcing a spicy ground beef dish topped with a cornmeal crust.*

1 tablespoon butter
1 medium-sized onion, chopped (about 1 cup)
1 pound ground beef
2 cans (15 ounces each) chili con carne (with beans or without)
1 can (15 ounces) red kidney beans, drained
1 teaspoon chili powder
1 box (8½ ounces) corn muffin mix
1 egg
½ cup milk

Preheat the oven to 400°F. In a large skillet, melt the butter over medium-high heat; sauté the onion and ground beef for 8 to 10 minutes, stirring occasionally, until the beef is browned. Drain any liquid, then add the chili, beans, and chili powder; mix well. Place in a 2-quart casserole dish that has been coated with nonstick vegetable spray. In a medium-sized bowl, combine the corn muffin mix with the egg and milk. Pour the mixture over the chili. Bake for 25 to 30 minutes or until the center is set.

NOTE: If you want to make this an extra-hot tamale pie, add a dash or two of hot pepper sauce when you add the chili con carne.

# Award-Winning Veal Oscar

*4 to 5 servings*

*This is so tasty and easy, it sure is a winning Oscar!*

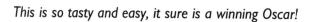

4 to 5 boneless veal cutlets (about 1 pound total)
¼ cup all-purpose flour
¼ teaspoon salt
⅛ teaspoon pepper
3 tablespoons vegetable oil
8 ounces crabmeat, flaked
1 box (10 ounces) frozen cut asparagus, thawed and drained
1 can (10¾ ounces) Cheddar cheese sauce

Preheat the oven to 350°F. Between 2 pieces of waxed paper, gently pound the cutlets to ¼-inch thickness with a mallet or rolling pin. In a shallow dish, combine the flour, salt, and pepper. Coat the veal with the flour mixture. In a large skillet, heat the oil over medium-high heat. Add the veal and sauté for 2 to 3 minutes per side. Place the veal in a baking dish that has been coated with nonstick vegetable spray. Top each piece of veal with the flaked crabmeat and asparagus. Pour the cheese sauce over the top. Bake for 25 to 30 minutes or until heated through.

NOTE: Have boneless chicken breasts instead of veal? *Voilà!* You have Chicken Oscar.

# Hand-Me-Down Chicken Favorites

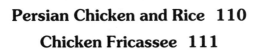

# Persian Chicken and Rice

*3 to 4 servings*

This comes from a small Middle Eastern country called Oman. It's been passed down and made easier along the way, and I thank the viewer who sent it to me!

2 tablespoons (¼ stick) butter
1 chicken (2½ to 3 pounds), cut into 8 pieces
1 medium-sized onion, chopped (about 1 cup)
⅓ cup chopped dried apricots (see Note)
⅓ cup raisins
2 cans (14½ ounces each) chicken broth
1 teaspoon salt
¼ teaspoon pepper
¼ teaspoon ground cinnamon
1½ cups uncooked long- or whole-grain rice

In a soup pot, melt the butter and cook the chicken for about 15 minutes, until brown on both sides; remove the chicken to a platter. Add the onion, apricots, and raisins and sauté over medium heat for 2 to 3 minutes. Add the chicken broth, salt, pepper, and cinnamon and bring to a boil. Add the rice and mix well. Return the chicken to the pot; reduce the heat to low, cover, and cook for about 25 minutes or until all the liquid is absorbed and the chicken is cooked through.

NOTE: I suggest using kitchen scissors or shears to cut the apricots into small pieces. If you dust them with flour first, it sure makes them easier to cut.

# Chicken Fricassee

*3 to 4 servings*

*For a treat, my family used to go to a little French diner once a month. We became friendly with the French owner, who always made us his family favorite. It's time to give this one a try at home! Thanks, Jacques.*

2 tablespoons vegetable oil
1 chicken (2½ to 3 pounds), cut into 8 pieces
1 can (10¾ ounces) cream of celery soup
½ cup milk
1 tablespoon lemon juice
¼ teaspoon ground thyme
1 bay leaf
½ teaspoon salt
¼ teaspoon pepper
1 medium-sized onion, chopped (about 1 cup)
2 medium-sized carrots, coarsely chopped (about 1¼ cups)

In a large skillet, heat the oil over medium-high heat and brown the chicken pieces on both sides, about 10 to 12 minutes. Remove the chicken to a platter and drain all but 2 tablespoons of the liquid from the pan. In a small bowl, whisk together the cream of celery soup, milk, lemon juice, thyme, bay leaf, salt, and pepper. Reheat the pan drippings over medium-high heat and add the onion and carrots; sauté for 3 to 4 minutes or until the onion is soft. Return the chicken to the skillet, pour the soup mixture over the chicken, and cover. Reduce the heat to low and simmer for about 30 minutes or until the chicken is no longer pink and the juices run clear. **Remove the bay leaf before serving.**

NOTE: Serve over cooked rice or noodles.

# Shortcut Chicken Cacciatore

*3 to 4 servings*

*Recently I ordered Chicken Cacciatore at a local Italian restaurant. Wow, was it tasty! But when I asked for the recipe, the chef rattled off about twenty ingredients and some complicated directions. Right then I knew I had to make my own version, so here's what I came up with. (Don't worry—it's got less than half the ingredients and half the work!)*

1 large onion
⅓ cup olive oil
2 cups sliced fresh mushrooms
2 cups thinly sliced red and/or green bell peppers
1 chicken (2½ to 3 pounds), cut into 8 pieces
1 jar (28 ounces) spaghetti sauce
½ cup water

Cut the onion in half, then into ¼-inch slices. In a large pot, heat the olive oil over medium-high heat. Sauté the onion, mushrooms, and bell peppers for 3 to 4 minutes or until just tender. Remove the vegetables to a medium-sized bowl, leaving any remaining oil in the pot. In the same pot, sauté the chicken pieces for 4 to 5 minutes per side or until lightly browned. Return the sautéed vegetables to the pot. Add the spaghetti sauce and water; mix well. Reduce the heat to medium-low and cook for 30 to 40 minutes or until the chicken is tender and cooked through.

NOTE: If you want to pep up your Cacciatore, maybe add ½ teaspoon dried basil or garlic powder, or turn up the heat with ¼ teaspoon crushed red pepper. The seasonings you add should depend on what kind of spaghetti sauce you use. Make your own adjustments. Also, remove the skin from the raw chicken, if desired.

# Chicken Cordon Bleu

*4 servings*

*A classic French dish that's quick and easy to make. Impossible, you say? Let me show you how you can surprise yourself and your gang...*

4 boneless and skinless chicken breast halves (1 to 1¼ pounds)
¼ teaspoon salt
⅛ teaspoon white pepper
¼ pound sliced Swiss cheese (6 slices)
¼ pound thinly sliced deli ham (4 slices)
½ cup flavored bread crumbs
Paprika for sprinkling

C'EST SI BON!! PARIS FRANCE

Preheat the oven to 350°F. Between 2 pieces of waxed paper, gently pound the chicken to ¼-inch thickness with a mallet or rolling pin. Evenly sprinkle each piece of chicken with the salt and pepper. Place 1 cheese slice and 1 ham slice on top of each chicken breast half. Roll up and secure each breast with a toothpick. Place in a 7" × 11" baking dish that has been coated with nonstick vegetable spray and sprinkle the chicken evenly with bread crumbs. Bake for 30 to 35 minutes, or until the chicken is cooked through. Remove from the oven and place ½ cheese slice on top of each chicken piece and sprinkle with paprika. Return to the oven for 3 to 5 minutes or until the cheese has melted. Remove toothpicks before serving.

NOTE: Regular styles of Swiss cheese and deli-style ham tend to be salty, so if you'd rather not add the extra salt, that's fine.

# Chicken Kiev Roll-ups

*6 servings*

*This Russian specialty has always been popular in restaurants, but it's rarely made at home because the traditional recipe calls for rolling and freezing and frying. The butter would often ooze out, too. Well, surprise! No oozing, and a simple way to make it yourself!*

1 tablespoon dried parsley flakes
1 tablespoon dried chives
½ teaspoon garlic powder
6 boneless and skinless chicken breast halves (1¾ to 2¼ pounds)
½ teaspoon salt
½ teaspoon pepper
3 tablespoons butter, cut into 6 equal slices
1 tablespoon seasoned bread crumbs, divided
⅛ teaspoon paprika

Preheat the oven to 350°F. In a small bowl, combine the parsley, chives, and garlic; set aside. Between 2 pieces of waxed paper, gently pound the chicken to ¼-inch thickness with a mallet or rolling pin. Sprinkle both sides of each breast lightly with salt and pepper, then sprinkle 1 teaspoon of the parsley mixture on one side of each chicken piece. Place a slice of butter in the center of each piece of chicken and roll each chicken breast tightly, tucking in the sides as you roll. Place the rolls seam side down in medium-sized muffin tins that have been coated with nonstick vegetable spray and sprinkle ½ teaspoon of the seasoned bread crumbs and some paprika over each roll. Bake for 25 to 30 minutes or until no pink remains and the juices run clear. Serve immediately.

# Today's Easy Chicken Paprikash

*8 servings*

*If more people knew how easy it is to cook Old World favorites like this one, there probably wouldn't be too many new favorites to try.*

8 boneless and skinless chicken breast halves (2 to 2½ pounds)
2 tablespoons paprika
1 can (10¾ ounces) cream of mushroom soup
1 cup sour cream
1 cup sliced fresh mushrooms
½ cup dry white wine
¾ teaspoon salt
¼ teaspoon pepper

Preheat the oven to 350°F. Place the chicken breasts in a 9" × 13" baking dish that has been coated with nonstick vegetable spray. In a medium-sized bowl, combine the remaining ingredients; pour over the chicken. Bake, uncovered, for 40 to 50 minutes or until a knife can be inserted in the chicken with ease and no pink remains.

NOTE: My family likes white-meat chicken, but this will also work well with chicken thighs and drumsticks. When using dark meat, you might have to add an additional 10 minutes to the cooking time.

# Neighborly Greek Chicken

*3 to 4 servings*

*There was a fairly large Greek population in my neighborhood when I was growing up, so I got to taste lots of really wonderful foods. This is a quick version of one of the most popular chicken dishes from my old neighborhood.*

½ cup olive oil
3 tablespoons lemon juice
2 teaspoons dried oregano
1 teaspoon dried parsley flakes
½ teaspoon salt
1 chicken (2½ to 3 pounds), cut into 8 pieces and skinned

Preheat the oven to 350°F. In a medium-sized bowl, combine all the ingredients except the chicken; mix well. Place the chicken pieces in the mixture and coat completely. Place on a 10" × 15" rimmed cookie sheet. Bake for 45 to 50 minutes, or until no pink remains and the juices run clear.

NOTE: If you want to give the chicken an extra zing and some great flavor, give it a squeeze of fresh lemon right before serving.

MR. FOOD®'S OLD WORLD
OOH IT'S SO GOOD!!™
COOKING MADE EASY

# Chicken Française

*4 servings*

*This is a popular dish on the French Riviera, in French restaurants around the world, and soon in your kitchen. What could be better—you don't even need a passport!*

4 boneless and skinless chicken breast halves (1 to 1¼ pounds)
¼ teaspoon salt
½ cup all-purpose flour
2 eggs, lightly beaten
4 tablespoons (½ stick) butter
⅓ cup dry white wine or dry vermouth
Juice of 1 lemon

C'EST SI BON!! PARIS FRANCE

Between 2 pieces of waxed paper, gently pound the chicken to ¼-inch thickness with a mallet or rolling pin. In a shallow dish, combine the salt and flour. Place the beaten eggs in another shallow dish. Roll the chicken breasts in the flour, then dip in the eggs. Melt the butter in a large skillet over medium-high heat. Cook the chicken for 3 to 4 minutes on each side, until golden. Add the wine to the skillet and squeeze the lemon over the chicken. Cook for 2 to 4 more minutes, or until the chicken is cooked through and the sauce begins to glaze the chicken breasts.

NOTE: This is also super with thinly sliced veal in place of the chicken.

# Chicken Stroganoff

*4 servings*

*This is a great way to use leftover chicken. And like so many Old World specialties, it has a rich, creamy sauce. Boy, do I love that!*

2 tablespoons (¼ stick) butter
1 can (4 ounces) sliced mushrooms, drained
¼ cup cooking sherry or dry white wine
½ teaspoon dried thyme
1 teaspoon seasoned salt
2 cups cubed cooked chicken (about ½ pound)
1 cup sour cream

In a medium-sized skillet, melt the butter over medium heat; add the mushrooms, sherry, thyme, and seasoned salt and cook for 2 to 3 minutes or until thoroughly warmed. Add the chicken and bring the mixture to a boil; reduce the heat to low, and simmer for 10 minutes, stirring occasionally. Remove from the heat and stir in the sour cream.

NOTE: Serve this over 1 pound of cooked egg noodles.

# Moroccan Chicken

*6 servings*

*Some friends recently returned from a tour to Morocco and couldn't wait to share this recipe with me. Now I get to share it with you!*

½ cup all-purpose flour
2 tablespoons sugar
2 tablespoons ground cinnamon
½ teaspoon salt
½ cup finely chopped blanched almonds
2 eggs, beaten
6 boneless and skinless chicken breast halves (1½ to 2 pounds)
3 tablespoons vegetable oil
½ cup orange marmalade
¼ cup orange juice
¼ cup sliced blanched almonds for sprinkling

In a shallow bowl, combine the flour, sugar, cinnamon, salt, and chopped almonds; set aside. Place the eggs in another shallow bowl. Dip the chicken into the beaten eggs, then coat with the flour mixture. In a large skillet, over medium-high heat, heat the oil until hot; do not burn. Sauté the chicken for about 4 minutes per side or until golden. In a small bowl, combine the marmalade and orange juice; spoon evenly over the chicken. Cover and reduce the heat to low; simmer for about 5 minutes or until the chicken is cooked through. Sprinkle the sliced almonds over the top and serve immediately.

# Tandoori Chicken

*3 to 4 servings*

*A tandoor is a hole dug in the ground surrounded by hot coals to create an oven. And one of the most well-known chicken dishes is one that was created in this type of Indian oven. (Don't worry—you don't have to dig a hole in your backyard to make my version!)*

1½ cups plain yogurt
1 teaspoon ground ginger
1 teaspoon ground cumin
1 teaspoon crushed red pepper
1 teaspoon salt
½ teaspoon garlic powder
1 teaspoon paprika
½ teaspoon ground coriander
⅛ teaspoon ground cloves
⅛ teaspoon black pepper
2 tablespoons hot pepper sauce
8 to 10 drops red food color
1 chicken (2½ to 3 pounds), cut into 8 pieces

Preheat the oven to 350°F. Place all the ingredients except the chicken in a medium-sized bowl; mix well. Coat the chicken with the mixture and place on a baking sheet that has been coated with nonstick vegetable spray. Bake for 45 to 50 minutes, or until the juices run clear and no pink remains.

NOTE: Serve this with Indian Refresher Salad (page 41). It's a cool way to take the edge off the hot pepper sauce in the chicken!

# Chicken à l'Orange

*3 to 4 servings*

*Over the years, French cooking has gained a reputation for being really complicated. Well, it's not true when Monsieur Food makes it!*

1 chicken (2½ to 3 pounds), cut into 8 pieces
1 jar (12 ounces) orange marmalade
½ teaspoon salt
⅛ teaspoon cayenne pepper
1 can (11 ounces) mandarin oranges, drained

Preheat the oven to 350°F. Place the chicken in a 9" × 13" baking dish that has been coated with nonstick vegetable spray. Combine the remaining ingredients in a medium-sized bowl. Spread the mixture over the chicken and bake, uncovered, for 50 to 60 minutes or until a fork can be inserted into the chicken with ease and no pink remains.

NOTE: Make sure you don't miss any of the flavor—serve the drippings and sauce over the chicken.

# Greek Isles Chicken Salad Pitas

*4 servings*

*I haven't been to Greece yet (and I hope I can get there soon), but I hear that the island breeze is always fresh and exciting. That fits with this recipe, 'cause it's also fresh and exciting!*

1 tablespoon olive oil
2 teaspoons lemon juice
1½ teaspoons dried oregano
¼ teaspoon salt
¼ teaspoon pepper
2 cups cooked chicken chunks (about ½ pound)
1 can (2¼ ounces) sliced black olives, drained (½ cup)
½ cup (2 ounces) crumbled feta cheese
4 pitas

In a medium-sized bowl, combine the olive oil, lemon juice, oregano, salt, and pepper; mix well. Mix in the chicken and the black olives until well coated. Add the feta cheese and toss lightly. Cut the top off each pita bread and place ¼ of the mixture inside each. If you'd like to serve these warm, place them on a cookie sheet in a 325°F. oven for 15 minutes.

NOTE: Just before serving, you may want to add some chopped tomatoes and/or lettuce.

# Chicken "Schnitzel" with Mushroom Sauce

*4 servings*

*When you tell them what's for dinner, your family will probably ask you, "What's a schnitzel chicken?" Instead of answering, just have them taste!*

4 boneless and skinless chicken breast halves (1 to 1¼ pounds)
2 tablespoons (¼ stick) butter
1 can (4 ounces) mushroom stems and pieces, drained
1 can (10¾ ounces) cream of mushroom soup
¼ cup milk
2 tablespoons dry white wine
½ teaspoon onion powder
¼ teaspoon white pepper
1½ teaspoons dried parsley flakes (optional)
Olive oil for frying
2 eggs, lightly beaten
1 cup seasoned bread crumbs

Between 2 pieces of waxed paper, gently pound the chicken to ¼-inch thickness with a mallet or rolling pin; set aside. In a medium-sized saucepan, over medium-high heat, melt the butter and sauté the mushrooms for 2 to 3 minutes, until lightly browned. Add the soup, milk, wine, onion powder, pepper, and parsley and bring to a boil. Reduce the heat to low and simmer for 4 to 5 minutes. Cover and keep warm over very low heat. In a large skillet, heat the oil over medium-high heat. Place the eggs in a shallow dish and the bread crumbs in another shallow dish. Dip the flattened chicken in the egg, then in the bread crumbs and fry the chicken, 2 pieces at a time, for 4 to 5 minutes per side, until golden brown on both sides and no pink remains. Remove the chicken and drain on paper towels. Place on a serving dish and serve immediately, topped with the warm sauce.

# Chicken and Couscous

*4 servings*

*How 'bout giving a today twist to the Middle Eastern couscous tossed with chicken and vegetables? It's a true peacemaker around my table.*

⅓ cup olive oil
2 garlic cloves, minced
4 to 5 boneless and skinless chicken breast halves (1 to 1¼ pounds), cut into 1-inch pieces
1 medium-sized red bell pepper, diced (about 1 cup)
1 medium-sized onion, chopped (about 1 cup)
1 can (14½ ounces) chicken broth
½ cup water
3 tablespoons chopped fresh parsley
½ teaspoon ground cumin
1 teaspoon salt
¼ teaspoon pepper
1 package (10 ounces) couscous

In a large skillet, heat the oil over medium-high heat and cook the garlic for 1 minute. Add the chicken, red pepper, and onion. Sauté for 8 to 10 minutes or until the chicken is lightly browned on both sides, stirring occasionally. Add the chicken broth, water, parsley, cumin, salt, and pepper. Bring to a boil and stir in the couscous. Cover and remove from heat. Let stand for 5 to 10 minutes, or until the water is absorbed. Serve immediately.

NOTE: If you have any of this left over, simply reheat it in the microwave or in a skillet with a little more water or chicken broth.

# African Chicken Wings

*60 to 70 pieces*

*Sure, Buffalo wings are a rage today, but our African ancestors had their own type of hot flavors. And when we use those to flavor today-popular wings . . . Wow!*

½ cup (1 stick) butter, melted
½ cup olive oil
2 tablespoons crushed red pepper
⅔ cup lemon juice
4 large garlic cloves, crushed
2 teaspoons ground black pepper
5 to 6 pounds split chicken wings or drumettes

Preheat the oven to 400°F. In a large bowl, combine all the ingredients except the chicken wings; mix well. Rinse and pat dry the chicken wings and place in the sauce; toss to coat well. Place on rimmed cookie sheets that have been coated with nonstick vegetable spray and bake for 45 to 50 minutes or until done to desired crispness.

NOTE: Wanna have your whole party doing a dance? Add a bit more crushed red pepper to this. It sure will add extra zing! And if you want to start with whole wings and split them yourself before cooking, split them at each joint and discard the tips. This makes them so much easier to eat.

# Countryside Chicken

*3 to 4 servings*

*Originally, the French called a dish similar to this cassoulet. Well, I've short-ened it up a bit and it still reminds me of a hearty, flavorful poultry dish you might find served in the French countryside.*

2 tablespoons olive oil
2 pounds chicken thighs or drumsticks (about 8 pieces)
1 medium-sized onion, chopped (about 1 cup)
1 can (28 ounces) whole tomatoes, drained and chopped
2 tablespoons tomato paste
1 tablespoon dried parsley flakes
2 teaspoons garlic powder
¼ teaspoon crushed red pepper
2 cans (14 to 16 ounces each) cannellini beans
(white kidney beans), drained

Heat the olive oil over medium heat in a large skillet. Brown the chicken for 10 minutes on each side. Add the onion and sauté for about 2 minutes. Drain excess liquid. In a medium-sized bowl, com-bine the remaining ingredients and add to the chicken. Reduce the heat to low, and simmer for 20 minutes, until the chicken is tender and cooked through.

NOTE: You can use any type of white bean here in place of the cannellini beans . . . you know, garbanzo beans (chick peas), black-eyed peas, or others.

*C'EST SI BON!!*
*PARIS*
*FRANCE*

# Wined and Dined Chicken

*3 to 4 servings*

*Sometimes you want a chicken dish that's a bit fancy-tasting, without all the fancy work and cleanup. Well, this one fits the bill... and you don't have to worry about the alcohol in the wine because it should disappear during the cooking.*

1 chicken (2½ to 3 pounds), cut into 8 pieces
½ cup all-purpose flour
2 tablespoons vegetable oil
1 small onion, chopped (about ½ cup)
3 cups sliced fresh mushrooms (½ pound)
1 cup chicken broth
½ cup dry red wine
1½ teaspoons salt
¼ teaspoon pepper
1 bay leaf
2 tablespoons dried parsley flakes

Place the chicken in a resealable plastic bag. Add the flour and shake to lightly dust the chicken. Heat the oil over medium-high heat in a large skillet. Cook the chicken for about 10 minutes, turning occasionally to lightly brown both sides. Remove the chicken to a platter. Add the onion and mushrooms to the skillet and sauté for 4 to 5 minutes or until tender. Add the chicken broth and wine to the onion and mushroom mixture. Add the salt, pepper, bay leaf, and parsley; mix well. Return the chicken to the skillet, cover, and simmer for 30 to 40 minutes or until the chicken is tender and cooked through. **Remove the bay leaf before serving.**

NOTE: If you prefer to be "wined and dined" without the wine, simply replace it with ½ cup of either nonalcoholic wine or apple juice.

# Tempting Tastes
# of the Seas

# Bullfighter's Shrimp

*3 to 4 servings*

*Most of us wouldn't be willing to jump into the ring with a wild bull—but everybody will be jumping in line for seconds of this Spanish favorite!*

2 cans (14½ ounces each) Italian stewed tomatoes
2 tablespoons red wine vinegar
1 medium-sized green bell pepper, cut into thin strips
1 small onion, chopped (about ½ cup)
1 to 1¼ pounds raw shrimp, peeled and deveined
¼ teaspoon cayenne pepper

In a medium-sized saucepan, combine the tomatoes, vinegar, green pepper, and onion. Bring to a boil, then simmer over medium-low heat for 10 minutes. Reduce the heat to low. Add the shrimp and cayenne pepper and let simmer for 10 minutes more, or until the shrimp are pink, tender, and completely cooked.

NOTE: I like to serve this over a hearty mound of cooked rice or pasta!!

# Pacific Salmon

*4 servings*

*Once you taste this combination of salmon and Asian seasonings, you'll know you've got a new family favorite.*

⅓ cup teriyaki sauce
⅓ cup apricot preserves
¼ teaspoon ground ginger
1 garlic clove, minced
3 tablespoons chopped scallion
4 salmon steaks (6 ounces each)

In a small saucepan, combine all the ingredients except the salmon; mix well. Bring to a boil over high heat, then reduce the heat to low and simmer for 1 minute; set aside to cool completely. Place the salmon in a 9" × 13" baking dish that has been coated with nonstick vegetable spray. Pour the cooled marinade over the salmon, turning to coat both sides. Cover and marinate in the refrigerator for 10 minutes; turn the steaks over, cover, and marinate in the refrigerator for another 10 minutes. Remove the salmon from the dish and discard the marinade. Grill over medium-high heat or in a preheated broiler at its highest setting for 6 to 9 minutes (turning once after 4 minutes), or until the salmon flakes easily with a fork.

NOTE: You can use either salmon fillets or steaks—whichever is on sale.

# Homestyle Coquilles St.-Jacques

*4 to 6 servings*

*Don't let the name scare you! Sure, you've seen this French dish on restaurant menus, but why wait to go out to try this seafood classic?*

4 tablespoons (½ stick) butter
1 pound fresh mushrooms, cleaned and cut into quarters
1½ pounds sea or bay scallops
½ pint heavy cream
2 eggs, beaten
¼ cup dry white wine
1 tablespoon lemon juice
½ teaspoon salt
¼ teaspoon white pepper
3 tablespoons seasoned bread crumbs

In a large skillet, heat the butter over medium heat. Add the mushrooms and sauté for 3 to 4 minutes. Add the scallops and continue to sauté for 4 to 5 more minutes, or until the scallops begin to turn white. (Bay scallops will take just 3 to 4 minutes because they're smaller than sea scallops.) With a slotted spoon, remove the scallops and mushrooms to a medium-sized bowl and keep warm, leaving the liquid in the skillet. Reduce the heat to medium-low and slowly add the cream to the skillet. Whisk the eggs into the cream. In a small bowl, combine the wine, lemon juice, salt, and pepper; slowly whisk this mixture into the cream mixture. Reduce the heat to low, return the drained scallops and mushrooms to the skillet, and heat through. Preheat the broiler. Place the scallop mixture in an 8-inch square baking dish. Top with the bread crumbs and broil for 2 to 3 minutes or until golden. Serve immediately.

NOTE: If the mixture is heated too long or on too high a heat, the sauce may curdle.

# Shrimp 'N' Pasta

*4 servings*

*Here's a hand-me-down recipe that's a one-dish meal. It's bound to be a family pleaser. And it's sure to please you 'cause it's easy to make but fancy-looking to serve.*

8 ounces rigatoni or other favorite pasta shape
¼ cup olive oil
1 pound cooked medium-sized shrimp, peeled and deveined
1 medium-sized green bell pepper, cut into short, thin strips
1 medium-sized yellow bell pepper, cut into short, thin strips
1 cup sliced mushrooms
3 garlic cloves, minced
1 tablespoon dried basil
2 medium-sized tomatoes, coarsely chopped
1 cup picante sauce
Grated Parmesan cheese

Cook the pasta according to package directions; drain. Meanwhile, heat the oil in a large skillet over medium-high heat. Add the shrimp, peppers, mushrooms, garlic, and basil. Cook for 3 to 4 minutes, stirring frequently, until the shrimp are warmed through and the peppers are almost tender. Stir in the tomatoes and picante sauce; simmer for 2 to 3 more minutes, or until warmed through, stirring frequently. Transfer to a large bowl, then add the cooked pasta and mix well. Serve with the grated cheese and additional picante sauce, if desired.

# Salmon Foldover Pie

*6 servings*

*When we're in a rush, we can enjoy this 1-2-3 version of Norwegian salmon pie made with canned salmon.*

2 tablespoons (¼ stick) butter
1 medium-sized onion, chopped (about 1 cup)
1 celery stalk, chopped (⅓ cup)
1 teaspoon dried dill
1 can (10¾ ounces) cream of mushroom soup
1 can (15½ ounces) pink or red salmon, drained and flaked
2 eggs, used individually
1¼ cups dry bread crumbs
2 unbaked refrigerated 9-inch pie crusts (one 15-ounce package)

Preheat the oven to 375°F. In a large skillet, heat the butter over medium-high heat. Sauté the onion and celery for 5 to 8 minutes, or until soft. Remove from the heat and add the dill, soup, salmon, 1 egg, and bread crumbs; mix until well combined. Place each pie shell on a cookie sheet that has been coated with nonstick vegetable spray. Place half of the salmon mixture on one side of each pie shell, about 1 inch from the edge. Beat the remaining egg, then brush the edges of the dough with it. Fold the dough over the salmon and pinch the edges together to seal. Brush the dough with the egg and bake for 30 to 35 minutes, or until golden brown and the center is hot.

NOTE: Red salmon gives a better color, but it is a bit pricier than pink . . . so go ahead and try both colors to see which is your favorite.

# Shrimp Egg Foo Yung

*12 to 14 servings*

*You can call these omelets or pancakes, but whatever you call them, they're a Chinese favorite that's popular at my house—for brunch and dinner!*

¼ cup vegetable oil, divided
1 can (4¼ ounces) broken shrimp, drained
5 ounces (half a 10-ounce package) frozen chopped broccoli,
thawed and drained
2 tablespoons chopped scallion
¼ cup chopped fresh mushrooms
3 tablespoons all-purpose flour
2 tablespoons soy sauce
4 eggs

啊!很好吃!
BEIJING
CHINA

In a large skillet, heat 1 tablespoon of the oil over medium-high heat. Add the shrimp, broccoli, scallion, and mushrooms and stir-fry until heated through; remove from the heat. Stir in the flour and soy sauce; set aside to cool. Meanwhile, in a medium-sized bowl, beat the eggs well. Stir the cooled shrimp mixture into the eggs and toss to coat. In the same skillet, heat 1 tablespoon of the vegetable oil over medium-high heat. Drop in the shrimp mixture by heaping tablespoonfuls, forming 3-inch pancakes, and cook for 2 minutes on each side, or until golden brown. Repeat the process, adding an additional tablespoon of oil for each batch of pancakes or as needed.

NOTE: Why not make an easy Chinese meal with Chinatown Hot 'N' Sour Soup (page 21) and this.

# Italian Seafood One-Pot

*8 servings*

*Here's a super blend of Mediterranean seafood that our ancestors made in just one pot. We can do it the same way today—which still means lots of flavor and little cleanup!*

3 tablespoons olive oil
¾ to 1 pound fresh or frozen skinless whiting, cod, or haddock
fillets, thawed if frozen, cut into 2-inch pieces
½ cup dry white wine
1 bag (12 ounces) frozen okra
2 large tomatoes, chopped
1 medium-sized onion, chopped (about 1 cup)
1 large garlic clove, chopped
1 tablespoon minced fresh parsley
½ teaspoon salt
1 pound cooked shrimp, peeled and deveined
1 pound cleaned fresh mussels (see Note, page 146)
2 cans (6½ ounces each) chopped clams with juice
1 loaf crusty bread

In a large pot, heat the oil over medium-high heat. Add the fish pieces and cook for 3 to 4 minutes, until lightly browned. Add the wine, okra, tomatoes, onion, garlic, parsley, salt, and shrimp. Bring to a boil, then reduce the heat to medium and cook for 4 to 5 more minutes. Add the mussels and the chopped clams with their juice and cover. Cook for about 4 more minutes, or just until the mussels open. Do not overcook the mussels. **Discard any mussels that do not open by themselves.** Serve with the bread for dunking.

# Shrimp Málaga

*about 3 servings*

*Málaga is a seaport on the coast of Spain where the people are so lucky! Why? Because they can get their shrimp right off the boats. And what better way to make our fresh shrimp than the way they make it there?*

⅓ cup olive oil
4 garlic cloves, chopped
1 bay leaf
½ teaspoon hot pepper sauce
⅛ teaspoon salt
1 pound raw shrimp, peeled and deveined

In a large skillet or wok, heat the oil over medium heat; stir in the garlic, bay leaf, hot pepper sauce, and salt. When the garlic sizzles, add the shrimp and stir-fry for about 3 minutes, or until the shrimp are pink, tender, and completely cooked. **Be sure to remove the bay leaf before serving.**

NOTE: Serve with crusty bread or over cooked rice.

# Almond Butter Sole

*4 to 6 servings*

*The world's oceans sure provide us with super fish, and when we flavor it with these Mediterranean flavors, we can provide our families with another reason to say "OOH IT'S SO GOOD!!™"*

1 cup all-purpose flour
½ teaspoon pepper
¾ cup milk
6 sole fillets (about 2 pounds total)
¾ cup (1½ sticks) butter, divided
1 cup sliced blanched almonds
Juice of 1 lemon
1 tablespoon chopped fresh parsley

In a shallow dish, combine the flour and pepper. Place the milk in a separate shallow dish. Dip the fillets in the milk, then in the flour mixture. In a large skillet, heat ¼ cup butter over medium-low heat; add half the fillets and sauté, turning after 3 to 4 minutes, or until the fillets are browned on both sides and they flake easily with a fork. Remove the fish to a heated platter. Repeat with the remaining fillets. Add the remaining butter to the skillet, then add the almonds and brown. Stir in the lemon juice and parsley, then pour over the fish and serve.

NOTE: The thickness of sole fillets will vary, and so will the cooking time—so make certain the fillets are cooked through.

# Stir-Fried Chinese Scallops

*4 servings*

*Chinese stir-fry cooking sure is quick! And with this sure-fire winner, you'll think you're in Shanghai in no time.*

¼ cup peanut oil
1¼ pounds scallops
3 garlic cloves, minced
1 medium-sized onion, cut into 8 pieces
1 large head napa or Chinese cabbage, cleaned and sliced
crosswise to about ½-inch thickness (about 8 cups)
¼ cup water
2 tablespoons soy sauce
½ teaspoon sesame oil
¼ teaspoon pepper
1½ tablespoons cornstarch

In a large skillet or wok, heat the peanut oil over medium-high heat. Add the scallops and garlic and stir-fry for 2 to 3 minutes. Add the onion and cabbage and stir-fry for 4 to 5 minutes more, or until the onion and cabbage are slightly tender but still firm. In a small bowl, combine the water, soy sauce, sesame oil, and pepper. Whisk the cornstarch into the mixture until smooth, then add to the skillet. Mix well and cook for 3 to 4 more minutes, until the sauce is thickened and the scallops are cooked through. Serve immediately.

NOTE: People often ask me which scallops I recommend. I don't, because it really depends on what you prefer. Have fun doing your own taste tests!

# English Crispy Fried Fish

*3 to 4 servings*

*No Old World cookbook would be complete without this English favorite! So here's the fish part. Now all you have to do is serve it with your favorite French fries, Mate.*

1½ cups all-purpose flour
1 tablespoon baking powder
½ teaspoon salt
½ cup vegetable oil, plus extra for frying
1 cup cold water
1½ pounds haddock, cod, or grouper fillets, cut into thin strips
½ teaspoon salt

In a medium-sized bowl, combine the flour, baking powder, and salt. Add the ½ cup oil a little at a time, stirring constantly until the mixture forms a large ball. Gradually add the water, stirring until the dough becomes the consistency of pancake batter. (If you want a thick crust, use less water.) In an electric frying pan, heat ½ inch of oil to 350°F. Dip the fish strips in the batter, coating completely, and fry a few strips at a time until golden brown; drain on paper towels and keep warm in a 250°F. oven. Add additional oil if needed to keep the original level while cooking the remaining fish strips.

NOTE: This fish can be served alone, with tartar sauce, or with malt vinegar—that's the real English way. It'll stay crispy in the low oven for an hour or two, so it's perfect for those times when you just might have to hold dinner in the oven for a while. If you don't have an electric frying pan, you can make this in a deep-fryer filled with oil as per manufacturer's instructions and fry until fish is golden brown and begins to float.

# Steamin' Mussels

*3 to 4 servings*

*New Zealand is a large producer of mussels from the South Pacific, so the New Zealanders sure know how to cook 'em. Make them their way for guaranteed sweet, plump mussels every time!*

1 can (14½ ounces) chicken broth
¼ cup dry white wine
1 teaspoon salt
¼ teaspoon pepper
1½ to 2 pounds cleaned fresh mussels (see Note)

In a large soup pot, over high heat, combine the chicken broth, wine, salt, and pepper; bring to a boil. Add the mussels, cover, and cook for about 3 to 4 minutes or just until the mussels open. Do not overcook the mussels. **Discard any mussels that do not open by themselves**.

NOTE: Whenever we cook mussels, they need to be cleaned first. To clean mussels for cooking, wash them under running water and scrub away any grit or barnacles with a stiff food scrub brush. Remove the black "beard" from each mussel by cutting or pulling it off.

# European Fish Stew

*4 to 6 servings*

*With all the oceans and seas surrounding Europe, it's no wonder fresh sea-food has always been popular there. And after we let our fish dishes simmer to "marry" the flavors, we can close our eyes and imagine we've taken a trip to the Continent.*

¼ cup olive oil
2 medium-sized onions, chopped (about 2 cups)
2 garlic cloves, crushed
4 celery stalks, chopped
1 can (28 ounces) crushed tomatoes
1 cup water
½ cup dry white wine
2 bay leaves
4 sprigs fresh parsley
1 teaspoon salt
⅛ teaspoon cayenne pepper
2 pounds fresh or frozen whiting fillets, thawed if frozen, cut into
1-inch pieces
1 pound cleaned fresh mussels (see Note, page 146)

In a large soup pot, heat the olive oil over medium-high heat. Add the onions, garlic, and celery, and cook until tender. Add the crushed tomatoes, water, wine, bay leaves, parsley, salt, and cayenne. Reduce the heat to low and simmer for 10 minutes. Add the whiting and simmer for 10 more minutes. Add the mussels and simmer for 4 to 5 more minutes or just until the mussels open. Do not overcook the mussels. **Discard any mussels that do not open by themselves. Remove the bay leaves before serving.**

NOTE: Serve with crusty bread for soaking up the sauce.

# Grapevine Sole

*4 servings*

*Grapes and fish?! It may sound crazy but, after all, we cook with wine, and wine does come from grapes. So why not give this nice French taste a try?*

¼ cup all-purpose flour
½ teaspoon salt
1 to 1¼ pounds sole fillets
4 tablespoons (½ stick) butter
¼ cup dry white wine
1 cup (about 35) white seedless grapes

In a small bowl, combine the flour and salt; mix well. Dust the fish on both sides with the flour mixture. In a large skillet, melt the butter over medium-high heat and sauté the fish for 4 to 5 minutes, turning once. Add the wine and the grapes. Cook for 2 to 3 more minutes, until the sauce has thickened and the fish flakes easily with a fork. Serve immediately.

# Onion-Crusted Salmon

*4 servings*

*Salmon sure is popular in Norway. And when we top fresh salmon with a crispy onion topping like they do there ... WOW!*

4 salmon fillets (6 ounces each)
1 can (2.8 ounces) French-fried onions
¼ teaspoon pepper
½ teaspoon ground thyme
1 teaspoon dried dill
2 tablespoons chopped fresh parsley
2 tablespoons (¼ stick) butter, melted

Preheat the oven to 350°F. Place the salmon in a 7" × 11" baking dish that has been coated with nonstick vegetable spray. In a food processor or blender, combine the remaining ingredients except the butter and process until the onions are in crumbs (about 5 seconds). Place ¼ cup of the onion mixture on each fillet and drizzle with the melted butter. Bake for 20 minutes or until the fish flakes easily with a fork.

# Potatoes, Rice, and Then Some!

# Spanish-Style Potatoes

*6 servings*

*In Spain these are called* papa fritas. *Your gang will probably call them their favorites . . . so plan on taking a bow!*

¼ cup olive oil
4 large potatoes (about 2 pounds), peeled and sliced ⅛ inch thick
2 garlic cloves, crushed
2 tablespoons chopped fresh parsley
2 teaspoons seasoned salt
1 teaspoon ground cumin

In a large skillet, heat the oil over medium-high heat. Add the sliced potatoes and garlic. Cover and cook for 8 to 10 minutes, stirring occasionally. Add the remaining ingredients; mix well and cook for another 5 minutes, mix again, then cook for another 2 to 4 minutes or until golden and tender.

NOTE: You can even make these without peeling the potatoes, so use red-skinned or white-skinned potatoes . . . the option is yours!

# Potato Pancakes

*5 to 6 large pancakes*

*So many people claim these as their own! And your taste buds and belly will be happy to claim them, too!*

4 medium-sized baking potatoes (about 1½ pounds),
peeled and grated
1 small onion, finely chopped (about ½ cup)
1 egg, beaten
½ cup all-purpose flour
1 teaspoon baking powder
½ teaspoon salt
¼ teaspoon white pepper
¼ cup vegetable oil

Put the potatoes and onions in a strainer. Press down on them with the back of a large spoon to extract excess moisture. (If they're still watery, wrap them in a clean dish towel and squeeze to extract moisture.) In a large bowl, combine the potatoes, onion, and egg; mix well. Gradually add the flour and baking powder, mixing well, and season with salt and pepper. Heat ¼ inch of oil in a large, heavy skillet over medium to medium-high heat. Using about ¼ cup of batter for each pancake, add batter to the hot oil, being careful not to crowd the pan. Fry until the pancakes are golden on both sides, turning once. (If you like them crisper, fry until they're flecked with brown.) Drain on paper towels and serve hot.

NOTE: Sometimes I like to use bread crumbs or matzo meal (or a combination) instead of flour.

# Caramelized Scandinavian Potatoes

*6 servings*

*We all grew up with sugar-coated dreams and visions of dancing sugar plums. In some Scandinavian countries, the children are lucky 'cause they grow up eating sugar-coated potatoes! Sounds good to me!*

½ cup sugar
1 tablespoon water
¼ teaspoon salt
2 cans (14½ ounces each) whole potatoes, drained and dried
with paper towels

In a nonstick skillet, over medium-high heat, heat the sugar, water, and salt until the sugar has melted and the mixture forms a light brown syrup, 5 to 7 minutes, stirring constantly. Reduce the heat to low, then add the potatoes, coating them with the syrup. Heat for 6 to 8 minutes or until the potatoes are heated through and evenly coated, stirring constantly.

NOTE: The syrup is **very hot!** Be careful when preparing and eating these. You may want to let them cool a bit before serving.

# Greek Potatoes

*5 to 6 servings*

*A lot of Greek food has a heavy Middle Eastern influence, and this recipe is no exception.*

⅓ cup olive oil
2 teaspoons dried basil
1¼ teaspoons dried oregano
1 teaspoon garlic powder
1 teaspoon salt
4 medium-sized potatoes (about 1½ pounds), scrubbed and cut into 1-inch cubes
1 to 2 tablespoons lemon juice (the juice from ½ lemon)

Preheat the oven to 400°F. Combine the oil, basil, oregano, garlic powder, and salt in a 9" × 13" baking pan. Place in the oven for 5 minutes. Add the cubed potatoes, tossing to coat with the herb mixture. Bake for 40 minutes, turning occasionally, until the potatoes are tender inside and crisp outside. Drizzle with the lemon juice and serve immediately.

NOTE: It's nice to grate a bit of lemon peel over the potatoes just before serving.

# Farm-Style Potatoes

*5 to 6 servings*

*We always hear about good old hearty farm-style meals. Well, now we can all look forward to coming home to these!*

5 medium-sized potatoes (about 2 pounds), peeled and quartered
¼ cup olive oil
2 garlic cloves, finely minced
1 can (15 ounces) crushed tomatoes
1 cup pitted ripe olives, halved
½ cup loosely packed basil leaves, coarsely chopped,
or 1 heaping tablespoon dried basil
¼ teaspoon salt
1 teaspoon pepper
½ teaspoon sugar
½ cup chicken broth
1 can (14½ ounces) whole tomatoes, drained and
coarsely broken

In a large saucepan, cook the potatoes in boiling salted water until tender; drain. Meanwhile, in a large skillet, heat the oil over medium heat; add the garlic and sauté for about 1 minute, or until light golden. Add the crushed tomatoes, olives, basil, salt, and pepper; cook for about 2 minutes, stirring occasionally. Add the sugar, chicken broth, and broken tomatoes and cook for 2 minutes, stirring occasionally. Spoon the sauce over the cooked potatoes. Serve immediately or keep warm in a 250°F. oven until ready to use.

NOTE: This sauce is great served over cooked rice or pasta, too.

# Irish Champ Potatoes

*8 servings*

*Sure, you'll feel like a champ when you serve this Irish specialty!*

4 cups water
2 cups chopped scallions (about 15 scallions)
¼ cup (½ stick) butter
1 teaspoon salt
3 cups instant mashed potato flakes
½ cup sour cream
¼ teaspoon pepper

In a large saucepan, over high heat, combine the water, scallions, butter, and salt and boil for 4 to 5 minutes. Remove from the heat and add the potato flakes; mix well. Stir in the sour cream and pepper.

NOTE: Ground black pepper will work fine, but I prefer ground white pepper to keep everything light-colored and let the bright green of the fresh scallions stand out.

# So-Easy Potatoes Lyonnaise

*4 servings*

*I can't fool you. You've heard of these before, but did you know how easy it could be to make them?*

4 medium-sized potatoes (1½ pounds), peeled and cut into
⅛-inch-thick slices
1 medium-sized onion, peeled and sliced very thin
1 teaspoon salt
½ teaspoon pepper
½ teaspoon paprika
6 tablespoons (¾ stick) butter

In a medium-sized bowl, toss the potatoes and onion with the salt, pepper, and paprika until well coated. In a large skillet, melt the butter over medium-high heat. Add the potatoes. With a spatula, gently turn the mixture to coat it well with the butter. Reduce the heat to medium-low, cover, and cook for about 30 minutes, turning occasionally with the spatula until the potatoes are fork-tender.

NOTE: Serve on a platter sprinkled with a little more paprika for an extra-fancy look.

# Nutty Potato Drops

*20 potato drops*

*If you're ready for a unique French dinner go-along, stop here! Or should I say, start here?*

2 cups water
1 tablespoon butter
1½ teaspoons salt
¼ teaspoon pepper
2 cups instant mashed potato flakes
2 eggs
1 cup Italian-style bread crumbs
½ cup sliced blanched almonds
Nonstick vegetable spray

Preheat the oven to 400°F. In a medium-sized saucepan, combine the water, butter, salt, and pepper over medium-high heat. Just before the mixture boils, add the potato flakes and stir until dissolved. Remove from the heat and allow to cool for about 5 minutes. Add the remaining ingredients except the vegetable spray; mix well. Drop the mixture by rounded tablespoons onto a large cookie sheet that has been coated with nonstick vegetable spray. Spray the potato drops with the spray and bake for 20 minutes or until golden.

NOTE: A perfect make-ahead side dish. The drops just need to be rewarmed on a cookie sheet in a 250°F. oven for about 20 minutes.

# Swedish Mashed Potato Pancakes

*8 pancakes*

*I knew a very good Swedish cook who always made these for her family. If they're good enough for her family, you betcha they're good enough for us!*

2 cups water
¼ cup milk
4 tablespoons (½ stick) butter
1 teaspoon salt
½ teaspoon ground cumin
1 teaspoon onion powder
2½ cups instant mashed potato flakes
2 tablespoons chopped fresh parsley
1 egg, beaten
2 tablespoons vegetable oil

Preheat the oven to 400°F. In a large saucepan, combine the water, milk, butter, salt, cumin, and onion powder. As soon as the mixture comes to a boil, remove the saucepan from the heat and add the potato flakes; mix until smooth. Add the parsley and egg and mix again until smooth. Form the mixture into 8 equal-sized patties. Brush both sides with the oil and place on a large nonstick cookie sheet that has been coated with nonstick vegetable spray. Bake for 25 minutes, turning once halfway through the cooking.

NOTE: Try making the patties half the size directed in the recipe and they'll be perfect for snacks or hors d'oeuvres.

# Mediterranean Potatoes

*5 to 6 servings (3 cups sauce)*

*Lots of seasoning, lots of "OOH IT'S SO GOOD!!™"*

1 tablespoon olive oil
1 medium-sized onion, chopped (about 1 cup)
1 tablespoon chopped garlic
1 teaspoon salt
1 can (28 ounces) crushed tomatoes, drained
½ cup dry white wine
2 teaspoons sugar
2 teaspoons Italian seasoning
¼ teaspoon hot pepper sauce
¼ teaspoon pepper
5 medium-sized potatoes (2 pounds), peeled and quartered

In a large skillet, heat the oil over medium heat; sauté the onion and garlic just until the onion is soft. Add the remaining ingredients except the potatoes and cook for 15 minutes. Meanwhile, in a large saucepan, cook the potatoes in boiling salted water until tender; drain. Place the potatoes in an 8-inch square baking dish. Spoon the sauce over the cooked potatoes. Serve immediately or keep warm in a 250°F. oven until ready to use.

NOTE: You can also serve this sauce over mashed or baked potatoes.

# Turkish Pilaf

*4 to 6 servings*

*Did you know that authentic Turkish rice pilaf is a bit sticky? Well, it is. So, for a nice change of pace, why not give this one a try... I bet your guests stick around for more!*

¼ cup (½ stick) butter
1 medium-sized green bell pepper, diced (about 1 cup)
1 cup sliced mushrooms (about 4 ounces)
1 large tomato, cubed (about 1¼ cup)
1 cup uncooked long- or whole-grain rice
1 teaspoon garlic powder
1 teaspoon salt
½ teaspoon pepper
1 can (10½ ounces) condensed chicken broth
¾ cup water

In a medium-sized saucepan, melt the butter over medium-high heat. Add the green pepper and mushrooms and sauté for 5 minutes. Add the remaining ingredients, stirring until blended. Bring to a boil, then reduce the heat to low. Simmer, covered, for 30 minutes or until all the liquid has evaporated.

NOTE: No fresh mushrooms? Use a 4- to 6-ounce can of sliced mushrooms—just drain them first. No green pepper? Try diced zucchini.

# Spanish Rice

*6 servings*

*"Olé!" That's what you'll here after your family tastes their first mouthfuls. Go ahead ... tell them you got the recipe from your old friend, Señor Food.*

2 tablespoons vegetable oil
1 pound lean ground beef
1 medium-sized onion, chopped (about 1 cup)
1 medium-sized green bell pepper, chopped (about 1 cup)
1 cup uncooked long- or whole-grain rice
2 teaspoons chili powder
1½ cups water
1 teaspoon seasoned salt
½ teaspoon ground cumin
½ teaspoon pepper
1 can (8 ounces) tomato sauce
1 can (14½ ounces) whole tomatoes, drained and chopped

In a large skillet, heat the oil over medium-high heat. Add the beef, onion, and green pepper, cooking until the meat is browned; drain liquid. Stir in the remaining ingredients; reduce the heat to low, cover, and simmer for 20 minutes or until the rice is tender.

NOTE: For a lighter touch, you can substitute ground turkey or veal for the beef.

SPAIN ¡AY ¡QUÉ BUENO!

# Ready-in-Minutes Risotto

*3 to 4 servings*

*In Italy, Risotto is almost as popular as pasta! It can be served as a side dish or a main course, too.*

2 tablespoons (¼ stick) butter
1 cup uncooked long- or whole-grain rice
1 can (10½ ounces) condensed chicken broth
1 cup water
4 scallions, chopped (about ½ cup)
¼ cup grated Parmesan cheese

In a medium-sized saucepan, melt the butter over medium heat. Add the rice and sauté until golden. Add the chicken broth and bring to a boil. Reduce the heat to low and simmer, covered, for 10 minutes, stirring once. Add the water and scallions and return to a boil, then reduce the heat to low and simmer for 10 more minutes. Remove from the heat and stir in the cheese until blended.

NOTE: You might want to make this even heartier by adding left-over cooked chicken or turkey chunks and having it as a main course that way.

# Easy French-Fancy Rice

*4 to 6 servings*

*I mentioned earlier in the book that French food doesn't have to be compli-
cated. Here's another example that proves that!*

1 large onion, diced (about 1¼ cups)
2 tablespoons (¼ stick) butter
2 cups cooked rice
2 eggs, beaten
1 cup milk
1 cup (4 ounces) shredded Swiss cheese
¾ teaspoon salt
¼ teaspoon white pepper
¼ teaspoon paprika
1 teaspoon dried parsley flakes

Preheat the oven to 375°F. In a large skillet, sauté the onion in the
butter until golden. In a large bowl, mix the sautéed onion with the
remaining ingredients except the paprika and parsley. Pour
the mixture into a greased 1½-quart baking dish and top with the
paprika and parsley. Bake for 20 to 25 minutes or until light golden
and heated through.

# Peanut Rice

*6 servings*

*Peanuts in rice?! Why not? That's not new in ethnic cooking, so why not try it? Bring home the taste of many cultures with every mouthful!*

3 tablespoons peanut oil
1 small onion, chopped (about ½ cup)
¾ cup chopped red bell pepper
½ cup unsalted peanuts
1 can (10½ ounces) condensed chicken broth
1⅔ cups water
¼ teaspoon sesame oil
½ teaspoon salt
½ teaspoon pepper
1½ cups uncooked long- or whole-grain rice

In a medium-sized saucepan, heat the peanut oil over medium-high heat. Add the onion, bell pepper, and peanuts. Sauté for 3 to 4 minutes or until the onion and pepper are soft. Add the chicken broth, water, sesame oil, salt, and pepper and bring to a boil. Add the rice; mix well. Reduce the heat to low, cover, and cook for 20 minutes. Remove from the heat and let stand for 5 to 10 minutes, until all the water is absorbed.

NOTE: Try cashews, almonds, or pistachios (my favorites) in place of the peanuts . . . or mix and match 'em.

# Orange Bread Pudding

*6 to 8 servings*

*One of my kitchen testers said, "It's a fruity side dish." Another one said, "No, no, it's a dessert!" Well, I think this Dutch recipe could be either, and it goes well with poultry and ham.*

13 slices white bread, cut into quarters
1½ cups orange juice
¼ cup (½ stick) butter
1 cup sugar
2 eggs
½ teaspoon grated lemon rind
¼ teaspoon ground cinnamon

Preheat the oven to 325°F. In a large bowl, combine the bread and orange juice and beat with an electric mixer until smooth. In a medium-sized bowl, cream the butter and sugar until light and fluffy; add the remaining ingredients and mix until creamy. Add to the bread mixture; mix well. Pour into a 1½-quart casserole dish that has been coated with nonstick vegetable spray and bake for 1 hour, until the center is set and puffy. Serve immediately.

NOTE: This really is best when served right from the oven.

# Great-Grandma's Kasha

*6 to 8 servings*

*If my great-grandma had had a range with a stovetop like we have today ... boy, would she have been thrilled! With this new way to make her old favorite, we have more time to re-create more of the Old World classics.*

1 package (8 ounces) bow-tie noodles
1 can (10½ ounces) French onion soup
¾ cup water
6 tablespoons (¾ stick) butter
1 cup kasha (roasted buckwheat)

Cook the pasta according to package directions and drain. Meanwhile, place the onion soup, water, and butter in a medium-sized saucepan. Bring to a boil and add the kasha. Cover and reduce the heat to low; cook for about 8 minutes or until the liquid is absorbed. Add the noodles to the kasha combination. Mix well, and continue cooking until heated through.

NOTE: Kasha can usually be found in the supermarket ethnic foods section or the bean and grain section.

# Moroccan Stuffing

*6 to 8 servings*

*Since Morocco is only a few miles from Spain, this is another chance for us to get the tastes of more than one culture in the same dish!*

3 tablespoons olive oil
1 medium-sized onion, chopped (about 1 cup)
1 cup chopped mushrooms (¼ pound)
⅓ cup (2 ounces) slivered blanched almonds
½ cup seedless raisins
½ teaspoon salt
¼ teaspoon ground ginger
1 can (14½ ounces) chicken broth
1 package (8 ounces) seasoned stuffing cubes

Preheat the oven to 350°F. Heat the oil in a large skillet over medium-high heat; add the onion, mushrooms, almonds, raisins, salt, and ginger and sauté for 6 to 8 minutes or until the onion and mushrooms are tender. Add the chicken broth and bring to a boil. Remove from the heat and add the stuffing cubes; mix well. Place in a 1-quart baking dish that has been coated with nonstick vegetable spray, cover, and bake for 30 minutes until the center is firm.

NOTE: This reheats well in the microwave.

# Polenta

*6 servings*

*This is as Old World as you can get! A change from potatoes and rice, this is filling, hearty, and easy to prepare—especially with the wide availability of cornmeal these days.*

4 cups water
¼ cup (½ stick) butter
2 teaspoons salt
2 cups yellow cornmeal

In a large nonstick saucepan, bring the water, butter, and salt to a boil. Slowly stir in the cornmeal with a wooden spoon. Reduce the heat to low and continue stirring constantly until the mixture is firm. Cover and cook without stirring for 15 to 20 more minutes, or until thick and the sides pull away from the pan. Serve immediately.

NOTE: If you use a nonstick saucepan, when set this will turn right out onto your serving platter. If it should lump a little when you add the cornmeal, stir with a wire whisk for 1 minute or until the lumps break up. If there are leftovers that harden, cut into ½-inch slices and pan-fry in a little butter or oil.

MR. FOOD'S OLD WORLD
OOH IT'S SO GOOD!!™
COOKING MADE EASY

# Old-Country Pastas

# Better-Than-Ever Lo Mein

*4 servings*

*They say we eat with our eyes first, then our mouths. If that's so, then this colorful Asian dish will sure fill you up ... twice!*

½ pound vermicelli or spaghetti
3 tablespoons peanut oil, divided
2 tablespoons sesame oil
3 tablespoons soy sauce
1 teaspoon sugar
1 teaspoon cornstarch
½ teaspoon ground ginger
3 garlic cloves, minced
4 scallions, chopped (about ½ cup)
½ cup diced red bell pepper

Cook the pasta according to package directions, drain, and set aside. Meanwhile, in a small bowl, combine 2 tablespoons peanut oil, sesame oil, soy sauce, sugar, cornstarch, ginger, and garlic. In a large skillet or wok, heat the remaining peanut oil over medium-high heat and add the scallion and red pepper; sauté for 1 to 2 minutes, then add the pasta to the skillet and stir-fry. Pour the sauce mixture into the skillet; toss well and cook until heated through and the sauce has thickened slightly. Serve immediately.

NOTE: What a great way to use up those extra bits of different fresh vegetables (you know, like broccoli, onions, pea pods, and beans)! Just cut them up and toss them in with the red pepper.

# Not-So-Traditional Noodle Pudding

*12 servings*

*I grew up with a sweeter version of this noodle pudding called* kugel. *It was full of cinnamon, sugar, and sour cream and was good with dinner or as a dessert. This version makes a better side dish for hearty meals like roasts, steaks, and roast chicken.*

1 package (16 ounces) egg noodles
1 package (10 ounces) frozen chopped spinach, thawed and
well drained
1 envelope (from a 2-ounce box) onion soup mix
6 eggs
1 can (10¾ ounces) cream of mushroom soup
¼ cup vegetable oil
¼ teaspoon ground nutmeg
1 teaspoon salt
¼ teaspoon pepper

Preheat the oven to 350°F. Cook the noodles according to the package directions (but without salt) and drain. Meanwhile, in a large bowl, combine the remaining ingredients; stir. Add the noodles and mix well. Pour into a 9" × 13" baking pan that has been coated with nonstick vegetable spray. Bake for 40 minutes or until the top is lightly browned.

Oy S'iz Azoy Geshmak!!

YIDDISH
YIDDISH

# Spoonfuls of Spaetzle

*4 to 6 servings*

*When I first tried these homemade German noodles, I thought they were great, but I wondered how anybody would have time to make them themselves. Boy, was I surprised to find out that making them is almost as easy as boiling water!*

3 cups all-purpose flour
2 teaspoons salt, divided
¼ teaspoon pepper
2 tablespoons dried dill or mixed herbs (like dried chives,
parsley, and basil)
4 eggs, beaten
1¾ cups milk

In a large bowl, combine the flour, 1 teaspoon salt, the pepper, and dill. Make a well in the center and pour in the beaten eggs and milk; mix by hand just until smooth. Fill a large pot half-full with water and add the remaining 1 teaspoon salt; bring the water to a hard, rolling boil over high heat. Over the pot, with a wide, slotted spoon, scoop out a spoonful of the batter and shake it lightly until it breaks into strands that fall into the water; the pieces of batter will congeal to form spaetzle. When the spaetzle float to the top of the water, remove them with the cleaned slotted spoon and drain on paper towels. Repeat until no batter remains.

NOTE: Add spaetzle to any soup to make it homemade-yummy, serve it with any meat or chicken dish, or simply serve warm spaetzle plain, with butter or gravy, or topped with cheese.

# Quick Madrid Pasta

*5 to 6 servings*

*Did you know that olives are popular in Spain? The growing conditions are ideal, which makes this abundant vegetable show up in so many traditional Spanish recipes.*

¼ cup (½ stick) butter
2 to 3 small onions, chopped (about 1½ cups)
8 ounces angel hair pasta (capellini), broken into 3- to
4-inch pieces
1 can (14½ ounces) beef broth
⅓ cup water
1 cup (one 5-ounce jar) salad-style olives, drained
¼ teaspoon pepper

In a large skillet, melt the butter over medium-high heat and sauté the onions for 2 to 3 minutes or until soft. Add the capellini and allow it to brown, stirring occasionally. When lightly browned, add the remaining ingredients; mix well. Reduce the heat to low, cover, and simmer, stirring occasionally, for about 10 minutes or until all the liquid is absorbed.

NOTE: This is off the record, of course, but if you're one of those people who's not crazy about olives, you can leave them out.

# Covered Lasagna Pizza

*6 to 8 servings*

*In the Old Country, they really knew how to make lasagna. And when we blend that Old World goodness with the fun and flavor of today's pizzas . . . Well, taste it yourself!*

12 lasagna noodles
3 cups (12 ounces) shredded mozzarella cheese, divided
1 package (3½ ounces) sliced pepperoni
1½ cups sliced fresh mushrooms
1 jar (14 ounces) spaghetti sauce

Preheat the oven to 375°F. Cook the noodles according to package directions; drain and pat dry with paper towels. Place 6 noodles crosswise on a 10-inch rimmed cookie sheet that has been coated with nonstick vegetable spray. (Cut the noodles to fit, if necessary.) Sprinkle 1¼ cups of the cheese over the noodles. Layer the pepperoni and mushrooms evenly over the cheese. Cover with 6 more noodles placed in the same crosswise direction. Spread the sauce over the noodles and sprinkle with the remaining cheese. Coat one side of a large piece of aluminum foil with nonstick vegetable spray and cover the pan with the coated side toward the lasagna (so the cheese won't stick); bake for 20 minutes or until the cheese is melted.

NOTE: After you try this you're going to designate one night a week as "Covered Lasagna Pizza Night"!

# Pierogi Magic

*12 servings*

*A good friend visited us recently and I have to thank her for sharing her Polish grandma's recipe. We turned it into a pierogi lasagna, and it's been turning out to be a big side dish hit with almost anything we serve!*

12 lasagna noodles
⅓ cup vegetable oil
4 to 5 medium-sized onions, finely chopped (about 3 cups)
½ teaspoon pepper
1½ cups (6 ounces) shredded Cheddar cheese
6 cups warm seasoned mashed potatoes (instant potatoes
are fine)

Preheat the oven to 350°F. Cook the noodles according to the package directions and drain; set aside. Meanwhile, in a large skillet, heat the oil over medium-high heat. Sauté the onions for 8 to 10 minutes or until golden brown. Reserve ½ cup onions for topping. Add the remaining onions, pepper, and cheese to the potatoes and mix well. Place 3 noodles on the bottom of a 9" × 13" glass baking dish that has been coated with nonstick vegetable spray. Spread the noodles with one-third of the potato mixture. Layer with 3 more noodles and continue until there is a total of 4 layers of noodles and 3 layers of potatoes (with a noodle layer on the top). Spread the remaining onions on top. Cover with aluminum foil and bake for 30 minutes or until heated through.

NOTE: You might want to add a few cooked sliced mushrooms to the potatoes, or maybe a cup of well-drained sauerkraut.

# Caraway Dutch Noodles

*6 servings*

*Cooking steak, pot roast, or a hearty veal dish? This is the perfect side dish.*
*Okay, it goes with chicken and fish, too!*

1 package (12 ounces) medium egg noodles
4 tablespoons (½ stick) butter
2 teaspoons caraway seeds
Juice of 1 lemon
1 teaspoon salt
¼ teaspoon pepper
½ teaspoon dried parsley flakes

Cook the pasta according to the package directions, then drain and place in a large serving bowl; set aside and keep warm. Meanwhile, in a medium-sized saucepan, melt the butter over medium heat. Add the caraway seeds and sauté for 3 minutes. Stir in the lemon juice, salt, pepper, and parsley. Pour the sauce over the cooked noodles and serve immediately.

NOTE: I try to use medium egg noodles that have a fluffy curled edge. It gives the dish a rich look.

# Our Own Gnocchi

*4 servings*

*Wouldn't it be nice to say you made it from scratch—pasta and all?! Well, now you can say that, and no, you don't need a pasta machine!*

¾ cup milk
¼ cup water, plus extra as directed below
½ cup (1 stick) butter
1⅓ cups all-purpose flour
¼ teaspoon salt
5 eggs

Fill a soup pot three-quarters full with water and bring the water to a boil. Meanwhile, in a medium-sized nonstick saucepan, over medium-high heat, heat the milk, ¼ cup water, and butter until the mixture boils, stirring occasionally. Add the flour and salt all at once, and stir vigorously until the mixture forms a ball in the middle of the saucepan. Remove the saucepan from the heat and allow to cool slightly, about 5 minutes. Add the eggs one at a time, mixing well after each addition. Drop the dough into the boiling water **½ teaspoon at a time**. When the dough balls (gnocchi) come to the surface, allow them to continue to cook for 1 minute. Using a slotted spoon, remove the gnocchi from the boiling water and place them in a large bowl of cold water; after about 1 minute, remove them from the cold water and drain well. Continue until all the dough is used; toss immediately with your favorite sauce.

NOTE: See the next page for a yummy cheese sauce to go along with your homemade gnocchi.

# Cheese Sauce for Gnocchi

*4 servings*

*Your friends won't believe you when you tell them how easy this is—they'll think you secretly went to Italian cooking school!*

1 can (10¾ ounces) condensed cream of chicken soup
½ cup milk
½ teaspoon onion powder
½ cup grated Parmesan cheese, divided
¼ teaspoon hot pepper sauce
⅛ teaspoon white pepper
¼ teaspoon paprika

Preheat the oven to 350°F. In a medium-sized saucepan, over medium heat, combine the chicken soup, milk, onion powder, ¼ cup Parmesan cheese, hot pepper sauce, and white pepper; mix well. Heat the mixture until hot but not boiling, stirring occasionally. Pour over cooked gnocchi; mix well. Pour the gnocchi mixture into a 7" × 11" glass baking dish that has been coated with nonstick vegetable spray and sprinkle with the remaining Parmesan cheese and paprika. Bake for 30 minutes, until hot and puffy.

NOTE: You could simply pour this sauce over cooked gnocchi and serve them like that, but for a nice casserole, follow the baking directions on page 179.

# Northern Italian Pasta and Eggplant

*3 to 4 servings*

*Make a double batch 'cause it's even better the second day...*

8 ounces penne pasta
¼ cup olive oil
1½ teaspoons dried oregano
1 small unpeeled eggplant, coarsely chopped (about 3 cups)
3 unpeeled ripe tomatoes, cubed
1 teaspoon chopped fresh parsley
1 teaspoon garlic powder
1 teaspoon sugar
½ teaspoon salt
¼ teaspoon black pepper
¼ teaspoon crushed red pepper
¼ cup grated Parmesan cheese

Cook the pasta according to the package directions; drain, set aside, and keep warm. Meanwhile, in a large skillet, heat the oil over medium-high heat. Stir in the oregano, then add the eggplant and tomatoes and cook for 3 to 4 minutes, stirring occasionally. Stir in the parsley, garlic powder, sugar, salt, and peppers. Reduce the heat to medium-low, cover, and cook for 10 minutes. Pour the eggplant mixture over the cooked pasta and toss with the Parmesan cheese. Serve immediately.

NOTE: You can make the sauce a few days before using it. Store, covered, in the refrigerator. Just heat and serve over cooked pasta.

# Greek Pasta Salad

*8 to 10 servings*

*I'm sure I've told you that just because a dish is made with pasta that doesn't mean it's got to be Italian. Check out this one if you need proof (and even if you don't)!*

1 box (12 to 16 ounces) radiatore or pasta ruffles
1 bag (10 ounces) fresh spinach, rinsed, dried, and
coarsely chopped
½ pound (8 ounces) feta cheese, crumbled
½ cup Italian dressing
½ cup vegetable oil
1 tablespoon chopped fresh basil or 1½ teaspoons dried basil
1 tablespoon grated Parmesan cheese
1 tablespoon wine vinegar
¼ teaspoon salt
¼ teaspoon pepper

Cook the pasta according to the package directions; drain and cool immediately by rinsing in cold water, then drain again. Meanwhile, in a large bowl, combine all the remaining ingredients thoroughly but gently; add the pasta and toss. Serve or refrigerate until ready to use.

NOTE: I like this best served at room temperature.

# Straw and Hay

*3 to 4 servings*

*Yup, it's a silly name—but when you see the finished dish you'll know how it got its name!*

2 tablespoons olive oil
2 garlic cloves, minced
2 cups sliced fresh mushrooms
1 cup sour cream
½ pint heavy cream
1 teaspoon salt
¼ teaspoon white pepper
6 ounces spinach fettuccine, cooked and drained
6 ounces egg fettuccine, cooked and drained
½ cup grated Parmesan cheese

In a large skillet, heat the olive oil over medium-high heat. Add the garlic and sauté briefly. Add the mushrooms and sauté for 4 to 5 minutes. Add the sour cream, heavy cream, salt, and pepper. Heat through, then add the cooked pasta and toss to coat evenly. Add the Parmesan cheese and mix well. Serve immediately.

NOTE: With the popularity of pasta today, you may be able to find a 12-ounce package of fettuccine florentine—a combination of spinach and egg fettuccine—in the supermarket pasta section. You can use that in place of 6 ounces of each of the other kinds.

MR. FOOD'S OLD WORLD
**OOH IT'S SO GOOD!!**™
COOKING MADE EASY

# Windmill Pasta

*6 servings*

*Just like a Dutch windmill goes 'round and 'round, this Dutch dish will go 'round and 'round your table. Why? 'Cause the gang will be asking for seconds and thirds and . . .*

1 package (12 ounces) wide egg noodles
2 tablespoons (¼ stick) butter
1 medium-sized onion, chopped (about 1 cup)
1 cup frozen peas
1 teaspoon salt
¼ teaspoon pepper
1 can (10¾ ounces) condensed cream of mushroom soup
2 tablespoons grated Parmesan cheese

Cook the noodles according to package directions; drain and set aside in a large bowl. Meanwhile, in a medium-sized saucepan, melt the butter over medium heat; add the onion and sauté until tender. Add the frozen peas and cook for 3 minutes. Stir in the salt, pepper, and mushroom soup. Cook until the mixture is bubbly and heated through. Pour the soup mixture over the cooked noodles and toss to coat. Sprinkle with the Parmesan cheese, and serve immediately.

NOTE: You might want to make this with frozen peas one time and frozen mixed vegetables the next. It'll keep your family guessing!

# Fettuccine Alfredo

*6 to 8 servings*

*If I had to choose the most popular Old World international dishes, this one would certainly be a contender!*

1 package (12 ounces) fettuccine
1 pint heavy cream
½ teaspoon pepper
2 eggs, beaten
½ cup milk
1 cup grated Parmesan cheese, plus extra for topping

Cook the pasta according to the package directions, then drain and place in a large serving bowl; set aside and keep warm. Meanwhile, place the cream in a medium-sized saucepan and heat over medium-low heat, about 6 to 8 minutes. Stir in the pepper. Using a whisk or fork, slowly add the beaten eggs to the cream, mixing constantly. Add the milk and 1 cup cheese. Continue mixing the sauce with the whisk until it thickens, about 4 to 5 minutes. Pour the sauce over the pasta and mix well. Top with additional Parmesan cheese, if desired, and serve immediately.

NOTE: Don't overcook this sauce because that could make it separate or curdle.

# Spaghetti Frittata

*4 to 6 servings*

*I hope to pass this one on to my kids and their kids, and so on. Not only is it tasty, but it's lots of fun to eat, too.*

8 ounces spaghetti
½ pound Italian sausage, casings removed
2 tablespoons grated Parmesan cheese
½ cup shredded mozzarella cheese
3 eggs
½ teaspoon salt
⅛ teaspoon pepper
2 tablespoons (¼ stick) butter
Spaghetti sauce for topping (optional)

Cook the spaghetti according to the package directions; drain and set aside in a large bowl. Meanwhile, in a large nonstick skillet, cook the sausage over medium-high heat for 5 minutes, stirring occasionally; drain. Add to the spaghetti along with the Parmesan and mozzarella cheeses; mix well. In a small bowl, beat the eggs with the salt and pepper and pour into the spaghetti mixture, tossing well. Melt the butter in the skillet over medium heat and add the spaghetti mixture. Cook for 5 to 6 minutes, without stirring, then place a dinner plate upside down on the skillet. Carefully turn the skillet over, flipping the frittata onto the plate. Place the skillet back on the burner and slide the frittata off the plate back into the skillet. Cook for 5 to 6 more minutes or until golden and cooked through. Slide onto a serving plate. Serve with warm spaghetti sauce or a little extra butter and salt and pepper.

# Vegetables
# They Grew Up On

# Hungarian Snap Peas

*4 servings*

*I know that Grandma would have loved having the conveniences we have in our kitchens today! So, we should enjoy using shortcuts like the ones in this recipe—the bacon bits and frozen snap peas.*

1 tablespoon vegetable oil
1 small onion, chopped (about ½ cup)
2 tablespoons bacon bits
1 package (16 ounces) frozen sugar snap peas, thawed
¼ cup sour cream
1 teaspoon paprika
½ teaspoon salt
⅛ teaspoon pepper

In a large skillet, over medium-high heat, heat the oil and sauté the onion until soft, about 2 minutes. Add the bacon bits and continue to sauté for another minute. Add the snap peas and cook, mixing frequently, for about 5 minutes or until the peas are heated through. Add the sour cream, paprika, salt, and pepper, and mix until well heated. Serve immediately.

NOTE: If you'd like, you can use green beans in place of the sugar snap peas.

# Spicy Caponata

*4 to 6 servings*

*Served as is, this is a hearty vegetable side dish. It's also a favorite appetizer salad for spreading on crackers or pitas. We should be thankful to the Old World cooks of Italy for this one!*

2 tablespoons olive or vegetable oil
1 large eggplant (about 1½ pounds), coarsely chopped
1 medium-sized onion, chopped (about 1 cup)
2 tablespoons garlic powder
½ teaspoon salt
1 can (8 ounces) tomato sauce
¼ cup white vinegar
⅓ cup firmly packed brown sugar
2 or 3 dashes hot pepper sauce

In a large saucepan, heat the oil over medium-high heat and add the eggplant, onion, garlic powder, and salt; sauté for about 5 minutes, until the eggplant begins to soften, stirring occasionally. Stir in the remaining ingredients and continue cooking over medium-high heat for 5 to 6 more minutes, until the vegetables are cooked well and begin to get mushy.

NOTE: If your eggplant is bitter, you may want to add an additional 1 or 2 tablespoons of brown sugar while it's cooking. You can eat this right away, but sometimes I make it in advance and keep it covered in the refrigerator for a few days before eating it. That way the flavors get to blend together and the taste is really rich.

# Onion Pie

*8 servings*

*Did the name stop you? No, it's not a dessert! It's a side dish that's a super go-along for meat, chicken, or fish. I got the original version of this from a viewer who is from Ireland, but I think it's a cross-cultural hand-me-down.*

One 9-inch (6 ounces) frozen pie shell, thawed
3 tablespoons butter
3 medium-sized onions, sliced (about 2½ cups)
2 eggs
1 cup sour cream
1 teaspoon salt
⅛ teaspoon pepper
¼ teaspoon ground nutmeg
⅛ teaspoon paprika

Preheat the oven to 350°F. Bake the pie shell for 8 to 10 minutes; set aside. In a 10-inch skillet, over high heat, melt the butter and sauté the onions for 3 to 4 minutes, separating the slices into rings; reduce the heat to medium-low, cover, and sauté for 1 to 2 more minutes. Remove from the heat. Place the sautéed onions in the prebaked pie shell. In a medium-sized bowl, combine the eggs, sour cream, salt, pepper, and nutmeg. Pour the mixture over the onions and sprinkle the top with paprika. Bake for 40 to 45 minutes or until the sides and crust are golden brown and a wooden toothpick inserted in the center comes out clean.

NOTE: Of course, this works fine with yellow or regular white cooking onions, but for a real knockout success, use sweet onions!

# All-Star Zucchini

*4 to 5 servings*

*Basil, garlic, tomatoes, zucchini... what an all-star line-up! And when you put them together in this Italian favorite, you'll be tempted to sing Italian love songs.*

2 tablespoons olive oil
3 medium-sized tomatoes, cut into small chunks (about 3 cups)
2 garlic cloves, minced
½ teaspoon dried thyme
½ teaspoon dried basil
2 tablespoons dried parsley flakes
1 teaspoon salt
½ teaspoon pepper
3 medium-sized zucchini, cut into small chunks (about 4 cups)

In a large skillet, heat the oil over medium heat. Add the remaining ingredients except the zucchini; cover and cook for 5 to 6 minutes, stirring occasionally. Add the zucchini, cover, and cook for 10 to 15 more minutes, stirring occasionally.

NOTE: You may want to serve this in a bowl, with some crusty French bread for dunking.

# Veggie-Stuffed Peppers

*4 servings*

*Almost every culture has some version of stuffed peppers. So, I'm not sure where they started, but I'm sure glad I discovered them! And since there's no meat in this recipe, these make a great side dish or a light main dish.*

2 bell peppers, split lengthwise, cored, and cleaned
¼ cup olive oil
1 medium-sized onion, chopped (1 cup)
4 garlic cloves, minced
1 ripe medium-sized tomato, finely chopped (1 cup)
4 to 5 anchovies, chopped
¼ cup chopped fresh parsley
½ cup dry bread crumbs
2 tablespoons dry white wine
¼ teaspoon pepper
Grated Parmesan cheese for sprinkling (optional)

Preheat the oven to 350°F. In a medium-sized saucepan, half-full of water, blanch the pepper halves for 4 to 5 minutes until they become tender but are still firm. Remove the peppers from the boiling water and plunge them into a bowl of cold water. In a large skillet, heat the oil over medium heat. Add the onion and garlic and sauté just until softened. Remove from the heat and add the remaining ingredients except the peppers and the Parmesan cheese; mix well. Fill the peppers with the mixture and place in a 7" × 11" baking dish that has been coated with nonstick vegetable spray. Sprinkle with Parmesan cheese, if desired. Bake for 20 to 25 minutes, or until heated through.

# Dill-Marinated Brussels Sprouts

*4 to 5 servings*

*Need a quick throw-together vegetable? Here it is . . . it's 1-2-3 easy and so different!*

¼ cup olive oil
1 tablespoon lemon juice
½ a medium-sized red onion, thinly sliced (about ½ cup)
½ teaspoon dried dill
½ teaspoon garlic powder
½ teaspoon salt
¼ teaspoon pepper
1 package (10 ounces) frozen Brussels sprouts, thawed
and drained

In a medium-sized bowl, combine all the ingredients except the Brussels sprouts. Add the Brussels sprouts and mix lightly. Cover and chill for 2 hours or until ready to serve.

NOTE: Make this in a glass or plastic bowl. The dressing would react with the metal in a metal bowl, giving it a metallic taste.

# Toss-Together Vegetable Salad

*8 to 10 servings*

*Give it a toss and you're ready to go. Now, that's my kind of cooking...
quick, tasty, and colorful, too!*

### MARINADE
½ cup red wine vinegar
½ cup vegetable oil
2 tablespoons chopped onion
2 tablespoons chopped fresh parsley
½ teaspoon chopped garlic
½ teaspoon salt
1 teaspoon sugar
¼ teaspoon black pepper

### SALAD
2 red bell peppers, cored and cut into eighths
2 green bell peppers, cored and cut into eighths
½ pound sliced mushrooms
½ cup pimiento-stuffed olives
1 head cauliflower, cut into large florets
1 cup large pitted black olives

In a small bowl, combine the marinade ingredients and set aside.
In a large bowl, combine the salad ingredients. Pour the marinade
over the salad mixture and toss to coat well. Serve immediately, or
cover and chill until ready to use.

# Stuffed Eggplant

*6 servings*

*Rumor has it that a Turkish woman experimenting in her kitchen created a recipe similar to this one. Her husband loved it and the recipe was passed around the countryside. Now I'm passing it on to you.*

2 medium-sized eggplants (about 1¼ pounds each)
4 tablespoons olive oil
2 medium-sized onions, chopped (about 2 cups)
4 garlic cloves, minced
4 large tomatoes, seeded and chopped (about 6 cups)
1¼ cups Italian-style dry bread crumbs, divided
1 teaspoon salt
1½ teaspoons pepper
¾ cup water

Preheat the oven to 350°F. Cut the eggplants lengthwise and scoop out the centers, leaving shells ½ inch thick and setting aside the insides. Brush the rims lightly with oil. Cut the eggplant insides into ½-inch cubes. Place the remaining oil in a medium-sized saucepan and sauté the onions for 5 minutes, until tender. Add the garlic and cook for 3 more minutes. Add the eggplant cubes and the tomatoes and cook for 8 to 10 more minutes. Add 1 cup bread crumbs, salt, and pepper; set aside. Meanwhile, place the eggplant shells cut side up in a 9" × 13" baking dish that has been coated with nonstick vegetable spray. Fill the centers with the eggplant filling. Top each shell with 1 tablespoon bread crumbs. Pour the water into the baking dish and bake for 45 to 50 minutes or until the insides are hot and the shells are tender.

# Red Sea Garbanzo Beans

*5 to 6 servings*

*Most of us just think of garbanzo beans as a special salad add-in, but when we serve them up with a Middle Eastern flair... watch out!*

1 tablespoon olive oil
1 teaspoon chopped garlic
2 cans (15 to 19 ounces each) garbanzo beans (chick peas),
drained
1 can (14½ ounces) stewed chopped tomatoes
1 teaspoon ground cumin
½ teaspoon salt

In a large skillet, over medium-high heat, heat the olive oil, then sauté the garlic until golden, about 2 minutes. Reduce the heat to low and add the remaining ingredients; cook for 15 to 20 minutes and serve immediately.

NOTE: If you prefer, you can serve this as a cold side dish.

# Spanish Spinach Loaf

*6 to 8 servings*

*You family's not crazy about spinach? Maybe with this Spanish-style creamed spinach loaf you'll change their minds.*

2 tablespoons (¼ stick) butter
1 teaspoon onion powder
½ teaspoon ground nutmeg
½ teaspoon salt
1 can (10¾ ounces) cream of mushroom soup
2 packages (10 ounces each) frozen chopped spinach, thawed
and well drained
1 cup dry bread crumbs
3 eggs, lightly beaten

Preheat the oven to 375°F. In a medium-sized saucepan, melt the butter over medium heat and mix in the onion powder, nutmeg, and salt. Add the soup, spinach, bread crumbs, and eggs; mix well. Pour the mixture into a 9" × 5" loaf pan that has been coated with nonstick vegetable spray. Bake for 1 hour or until a knife inserted in the center comes out clean. Allow to cool for 10 minutes, then invert onto a serving platter and cut into 1-inch slices.

NOTE: This is a perfect make-ahead dish. Just reheat it as needed.

# Swedish Not-Baked Beans

*6 to 8 servings*

*Of course, you like your regular baked beans, but why not try them with a Swedish touch when you want a change?*

3 cans (16 ounces each) kidney beans, drained
1 medium-sized onion, chopped (about 1 cup)
1 garlic clove, crushed
½ cup tomato sauce
1 tablespoon Worcestershire sauce
⅔ cup firmly packed light brown sugar
2 tablespoons molasses
¼ cup cider vinegar
2 tablespoons bacon bits
1½ teaspoons cornstarch
2 tablespoons cold water

In a large skillet, over medium heat, combine all the ingredients except the cornstarch and water; mix well and cook for 10 minutes. In a small bowl, combine the cornstarch and the water, then add to the bean mixture, stirring occasionally until heated through. Serve immediately or simmer until ready to eat.

NOTE: Light or red kidney beans? You choose . . . maybe some of each.

# Minty Indian Zucchini

*4 to 6 servings*

*Not too long ago, when I was at an international bazaar, I was lucky enough to try an Indian dish called* tabbakh ruhu. *It translates to "spirit of the cook," and after you taste it you'll know why—because everyone who eats it will compliment the cook, putting the cook in great spirits!*

2 tablespoons olive oil
4 medium-sized zucchini, cut into ½-inch slices (about 7 cups)
2 teaspoons chopped fresh mint or 1 teaspoon dried mint
1 teaspoon crushed garlic
¼ teaspoon mustard seeds
1 teaspoon salt
¼ teaspoon pepper

In a large skillet, heat the oil over medium-high heat and add the remaining ingredients. Stir until mixed and sauté for 15 minutes or to desired tenderness.

NOTE: There's so much zucchini available to us, especially in the summer, that we're always looking for a new way to make it. Your gang will like it . . . and so will your wallet!

INDIA
oh ye bahut
aeehaa hai!!
NEW DELHI

# Very-Stuffed Tomatoes

*6 servings*

*The Italians call these* pomodori ripieni, *which means "stuffed tomatoes."
I call these a perfect summer pick-me-up great for any time of the year!*

3 large tomatoes, cut horizontally, seeds and juice removed
and discarded (see Note)
½ cup dry bread crumbs
3 tablespoons grated Parmesan cheese
1 teaspoon chopped fresh parsley
½ teaspoon salt
⅛ teaspoon pepper
2 tablespoons (¼ stick) butter, melted
½ teaspoon Dijon-style mustard
⅛ teaspoon Worcestershire sauce

Preheat the oven to 350°F. Scrape out the centers of the tomatoes
with a spoon; chop the centers very fine and set aside. In a medium-
sized bowl, combine the bread crumbs, Parmesan cheese, parsley,
salt, and pepper; mix well. Add the chopped tomatoes, butter, mustard, and Worcestershire sauce; mix well. Place the cored tomatoes
into a 9" × 13" baking dish that has been coated with nonstick
vegetable spray and fill with the stuffing mix. Bake for 30 to 35
minutes, until the centers are hot but the tomatoes are still holding
their shape.

NOTE: To remove the seeds and juice from the tomatoes, gently
squeeze them after cutting horizontally. That's it! And if you use
seasoned bread crumbs you can eliminate the salt and pepper.

# Green Beans on the Side

*5 to 6 servings*

*Greek cooking uses lots of fresh beans, and they're often the focus of the meal. I like them, too, but I prefer these as a flavorful side dish.*

¼ cup olive oil
1 pound fresh green beans, trimmed
¾ cup water
2 tablespoons dried parsley flakes
2 teaspoons dried mint
1 teaspoon garlic powder
½ teaspoon onion powder
½ teaspoon salt

In a large skillet, heat the oil over medium heat. Add the beans and cook for 5 minutes, stirring frequently. Reduce the heat to low and add the remaining ingredients. Simmer for 15 to 20 minutes, stirring occasionally, or until the beans are tender.

NOTE: No fresh green beans available? Shucks! But don't worry . . . you can still make this recipe by substituting two 10-ounce packages of frozen cut green beans. Just thaw and drain them and cut down the simmering time to 8 to 10 minutes.

# Creamy Hungarian Mushrooms

*3 to 4 servings*

*One of my favorite recipes has mushrooms and sour cream . . . Mmm! Know which one it is? It's right here. You found it . . . now go ahead and make it! You'll be glad you did.*

¼ cup (½ stick) butter
1 small onion, thinly sliced (about ½ cup)
1 pound sliced mushrooms
½ cup sour cream
1 teaspoon paprika
½ teaspoon salt
¼ teaspoon pepper

In a large skillet, over medium-high heat, melt the butter and sauté the onion until lightly golden, about 6 to 7 minutes. Add the mushrooms and continue cooking for 8 to 10 more minutes, until tender. Reduce the heat to low. Add the remaining ingredients and stir until thoroughly mixed and heated through.

NOTE: Serve on steak, over cooked pasta, or as a different supper side dish.

# Spanish-Style Lima Beans

*4 servings*

*When I was growing up I never ate lima beans. I guess my mom never knew how to fix 'em. Well, here's a recipe for all moms and dads to try. I missed out on the yummy goodness of lima beans, but your kids won't have to!*

1 tablespoon olive oil
1 small onion, chopped (about ½ cup)
1 can (16 ounces) lima beans, drained
2 tablespoons chili sauce
¼ teaspoon salt
¼ teaspoon pepper

In a medium-sized saucepan, over medium heat, heat the oil and sauté the onion for 5 minutes, or until soft. Reduce the heat to low and add the remaining ingredients; mix well and cook for about 10 minutes, until heated through.

NOTE: The chili sauce gives the beans loads of flavor—with so little work and in so little time!

# Quick Creamed Spinach

*4 servings*

*Let's take a break from our traditional favorites of corn, broccoli, and peas, and give spinach another try. You never know, you might make a favorite of yesterday into a favorite of today!*

1 tablespoon butter
1 package (10 ounces) frozen spinach, thawed and drained
¾ cup sour cream
½ teaspoon onion powder
¼ teaspoon ground nutmeg
½ teaspoon salt
½ teaspoon pepper

In a medium-sized saucepan, over medium-high heat, melt the butter; add the spinach and stir until heated through. Combine the remaining ingredients in a small bowl and stir into the spinach. Cook, stirring, for another 1 to 2 minutes until creamy. Serve hot.

NOTE: A dash or two of hot pepper sauce will give this a whole new taste . . . so experiment!

# German Brussels Sprouts

*6 servings*

*What an authentic taste!! You can almost see the rolling hills as you eat them!*

2 packages (10 ounces each) frozen Brussels sprouts
1 can (10¾ ounces) cream of celery soup
2 tablespoons milk
1 teaspoon caraway seeds
¼ teaspoon salt
⅛ teaspoon pepper

Preheat the oven to 350°F. Cook the Brussels sprouts according to the package directions. Drain and place in a 1½-quart casserole dish that has been coated with nonstick vegetable spray. Add the remaining ingredients; mix well. Cover and bake for 25 minutes.

NOTE: Caraway seeds can usually be found in the supermarket spice section.

GERMANY
ACH DAS
SCHMECKT!!
BERLIN

# Sweet Memories

# Cappuccino Dessert

*4 servings*

*It's funny . . . I mention cappuccino and dessert in the same title, and every-body's eyes light up. Wait till you taste it! It'll sure wake up your taste buds.*

2 cups milk
2 tablespoons instant coffee granules
1 package (4-serving size) chocolate-flavor instant pudding and
pie filling
1½ cups frozen whipped topping, thawed
⅛ teaspoon ground cinnamon

In a large bowl, combine the milk and instant coffee. Add the pudding mix and beat with a wire whisk for 1 to 2 minutes or until well blended. Reserve 2 tablespoons of the pudding in a medium-sized bowl and divide the remaining pudding into 4 coffee cups or 4 to 6 individual glass dessert dishes. Mix the whipped topping with the reserved pudding and spoon the topping mixture over the individual servings of pudding. Sprinkle the tops with the cinnamon and refrigerate for 1 to 2 hours or until ready to serve.

NOTE: This dessert will really fool them if you prepare it in glass coffee cups!

# Black Forest "Quickie"

*18 to 24 servings*

*Just three ingredients? Is that possible? Yup, that's right. I've found the easiest way to re-create this German classic.*

1 package (18¼ ounces) devil's food cake mix
1 can (21 ounces) cherry pie filling
4 eggs

Preheat the oven to 350°F. In a large bowl, combine the dry cake mix with the remaining ingredients, mixing either by hand or with an electric mixer. Pour the batter evenly into a greased 9" × 13" baking dish and bake for 35 to 40 minutes, or until a wooden toothpick inserted in the center comes out clean.

NOTE: Almost any combination of cake mix and pie filling will work. Use your imagination to come up with your own favorite taste treats. And serve it plain, topped with whipped topping, or maybe try this:

# Black Forest "Quickie" Topping

*2 cups*

1 package (4-serving size) vanilla-flavor instant pudding and pie filling mix
1 pint sour cream

*continued*

In a medium-sized bowl, combine the dry pudding mix with the sour cream. Use immediately or refrigerate until ready to use.

NOTE: That's all there is to this "homemade" topping that's perfect for this or almost any cake. Why, it even works as a dip for holiday fruit platters!

# Dutch Dessert Pancakes

*4 servings*

*In Europe, a lot of people follow the tradition of eating salad after their main course. I guess the Dutch take that even further when they eat these dessert pancakes after dinner. Trust me . . . you'll be happy you've tried them, too!*

3 eggs
½ cup all-purpose flour
½ cup milk
2 tablespoons (¼ stick) butter, melted
½ teaspoon salt
½ cup confectioners' sugar
1 tablespoon lemon juice

Preheat the oven to 400°F. In a medium-sized bowl, mix the eggs, flour, and milk with an electric mixer; beat until smooth. Add the butter and salt and beat well. Pour the mixture into two 9-inch cake pans that have been coated with nonstick baking spray and bake for 10 minutes. Reduce the heat to 350°F. and bake for 5 to 7 more minutes, or until puffy and golden. Meanwhile, in a small bowl, whisk together the confectioners' sugar and lemon juice. Drizzle the glaze over each pancake and serve immediately.

NOTE: These are super topped with cut fresh fruit or canned pie filling. Yes, I've even seen them served with maple syrup. Have them your favorite way.

# Tres Leches

*12 to 15 servings*

*This Hispanic dessert is becoming really popular all around the country and I think that* Tres Leches, *Spanish for "three milks," translates to lots of* "OOH IT'S SO GOOD!!™"

1 can (14 ounces) sweetened condensed milk
1 can (12 ounces) evaporated milk
1 pint half-and-half
Pinch of salt
2 pound cakes (12 ounces each)
1 container (8 ounces) frozen whipped topping, thawed

In a large bowl, combine the sweetened condensed milk, evaporated milk, half-and-half, and salt; stir well and set aside. Cut each pound cake into 6 slices. Lay the slices tightly into the bottom of a 9" × 13" baking pan. Pour the milk mixture evenly over the cake slices, cover, and refrigerate for 2 to 3 hours. Spread the whipped topping over the cake and chill, uncovered, for another 1 to 2 hours. (There will still be some liquid on the bottom of the pan because this is more like a pudding than a regular cake and should be eaten with a spoon.)

NOTE: It's traditional to eat this plain, but I like to cover the top with fresh berries, other fresh fruit, or canned pie filling before serving.

# Overstuffed Napoleons

*12 to 16 servings*

*Everybody remembers seeing paintings of Napoleon Bonaparte, where he's got one hand inside his jacket. Hmm ... do you think he was hiding a Napoleon dessert in there? (They sure are good enough to keep to yourself!)*

2 puff pastry sheets (from a 17¼-ounce package)
2 packages (4-serving size each) vanilla-flavor instant pudding and pie filling mix
1½ cups milk
1 container (8 ounces) frozen whipped topping, thawed
Confectioners' sugar for topping

Preheat the oven to 400°F. Bake the pastry sheets according to the package directions; remove from the oven and allow to cool. In a medium-sized bowl, combine the instant vanilla pudding and milk. Beat with a wire whisk until thickened, then fold in the whipped topping. Spread the pudding mixture over 1 layer of the puff pastry. Place the other puff pastry flat side up over the pudding. Using a cookie sheet, press down lightly to evenly distribute the pudding and flatten the pastry just until the filling begins to ooze out the sides. Refrigerate for 3 to 4 hours or until ready to serve. Cut into serving-sized pieces with a serrated knife and sprinkle the tops with confectioners' sugar just before serving.

NOTE: Whatever you do, don't hide a piece in your jacket or you'll be sorry!

C'EST SI BON!!
PARIS
FRANCE

# Italian Dippers

*about 2½ dozen cookies*

*Imagine you just finished eating a big Italian dinner and you're looking for something to dunk in your coffee or milk. Well, that something is right here . . .*

4 eggs
1 cup sugar
1 tablespoon plus 1 teaspoon anise extract
⅛ teaspoon salt
2 cups all-purpose flour
2 teaspoons baking powder

Preheat the oven to 350°F. In a large bowl, cream the eggs and sugar until creamy. Add the anise extract. Slowly beat the salt, flour, and baking powder into the egg mixture until smooth and creamy. Drop the batter by teaspoonfuls about 2 inches apart, in oblong shapes, onto cookie sheets that have been coated with non-stick baking spray. Bake for 10 to 12 minutes or until golden.

NOTE: These will stay fresh for up to 1 week if kept in an airtight container.

# South American Raisin Cake

*12 to 16 servings*

*These days we expect to find convenience foods right on our supermarket shelves—and they make our lives so much easier! The idea for this recipe came from a traditional South American favorite. I bet the originators would have loved today's shortcut ingredients!*

1¼ cups apple juice
½ cup sugar
1 cup raisins
1 cup chopped walnuts
2 tablespoons cornstarch
3 packages (11½ ounces each) refrigerated cinnamon rolls
(8 rolls per package)

Preheat the oven to 325°F. In a medium-sized saucepan, over medium-high heat, combine the apple juice, sugar, raisins, walnuts, and cornstarch. Bring the mixture to a boil, then reduce the heat to low and cook for 5 more minutes or until the mixture thickens. Meanwhile, cut each cinnamon roll into 6 pieces. Place half of the pieces on the bottom of a 9" × 13" glass baking pan that has been coated with nonstick baking spray. Cover with the raisin-nut mixture, then top with the remaining dough pieces. Bake for 30 to 40 minutes, or until the dough is firm and golden. Cool, then cut into serving-sized pieces.

NOTE: For a sweeter touch, spread the icing from the cinnamon roll packages over the top just after removing the cake from the oven.

# Almond Torte

*12 to 14 servings*

*I'll share this recipe with you if you promise not to tell anybody how easy it is! It sure looks fancy, so let them think you worked on it all day!*

1 package (10 ounces) blanched almonds (2 cups), divided
1¼ cups (2½ sticks) butter
¾ cup granulated sugar
¼ cup firmly packed light brown sugar
1 egg
1¼ cups all-purpose flour
1 teaspoon almond extract

Preheat the oven to 350°F. Finely grind 1⅔ cups of the almonds in a blender or food processor; set aside. In a large bowl, cream the butter until soft with an electric mixer. Beat in the sugars until fluffy. By hand, mix in the egg, flour, almond extract, and the ground almonds; mix until smooth and stiff. Place the mixture into a 9-inch springform pan that has been coated with nonstick baking spray. Finely chop the remaining almonds and sprinkle them over the top. Bake for 50 minutes or until lightly browned and a wooden toothpick inserted in the center comes out clean. Cool completely on a rack before removing from the pan.

NOTE: It's best not to substitute margarine for butter in this recipe. And if you don't have a springform pan, you can use a 9-inch round cake pan.

# Italian Coffee Bombe

*6 servings*

*Layer after layer, spoonful after spoonful, you'll love this one. And with all its yummy pretty layers, it looks like a winner, too.*

¼ cup sugar
⅛ teaspoon salt
1 teaspoon all-purpose flour
2 egg yolks, beaten
½ cup milk
2 teaspoons instant coffee granules, dissolved in ⅓ cup warm water
1 tablespoon coffee-flavored liqueur
½ teaspoon vanilla extract
2 cups frozen whipped topping, divided

In a small saucepan, combine the sugar, salt, and flour. Add the beaten egg yolks, milk, and the dissolved coffee; mix well. Cook over low heat, stirring constantly, until slightly thickened. Remove from the heat, add the liqueur and vanilla, and stir; cool completely. Spread 1 cup of the whipped topping over the bottom and up the sides of a 1-quart bowl. Slowly pour half of the cooled liqueur mixture into the center of the bowl. Mix the remaining whipped topping with the remaining liqueur mixture and pour into the bowl gently and slowly. Cover and freeze for 3 to 4 hours or until firm. Remove from the freezer 20 to 30 minutes before serving. Carefully run a warm knife around the edges and invert onto a dinner-sized serving plate. Cut into small wedges.

# Not-Traditional Baklava

*14 servings*

*I've shortened the work, shortened the time, and shortened the cleanup of this traditional Greek dessert. One thing I didn't shorten is the taste!*

1 frozen puff pastry sheet (from a 17¼-ounce package),
slightly thawed
1 egg, beaten
1 cup chopped walnuts
½ cup honey
2 tablespoons (¼ stick) butter, melted

Preheat the oven to 400°F. On a lightly floured surface, with a rolling pin, roll out the puff pastry sheet into a 12" × 14" rectangle. Cut in half lengthwise and place on a cookie sheet that has been coated with nonstick baking spray. In a small bowl, combine the walnuts and honey. Spread half the mixture lengthwise along the center of each dough half. Using a pastry brush or paper towel, moisten the edges of the pastry dough with some of the beaten egg. Evenly fold the dough lengthwise over the filling. Seal the edges of the dough tightly by pressing the seams together with the tines of a fork. Brush the tops of both rolls with beaten egg and bake for 20 minutes. Remove from the oven and lightly brush the tops with the melted butter. Cool for 10 minutes before cutting diagonally into 2-inch pieces.

NOTE: After brushing the baklava with the butter, you can spoon the hot honey and butter drippings from the cookie sheet over the tops (before they cool).

# Strawberries and Cream Layer Cake

*8 to 12 servings*

*There's always room for this, because it's so light. It's like a Norwegian-style strawberry shortcake.*

1 package (18½ ounces) white cake mix
2 packages (10 ounces each) frozen strawberries, thawed and puréed
1 container (12 ounces) frozen whipped topping, thawed
1 cup fresh strawberries, cleaned, hulled, and sliced

Preheat the oven and prepare the cake mix according to the package directions, then bake in two 9-inch round cake pans. Remove from pans and cool completely, then cut each cake in half horizontally, making 4 layers. Place one cake layer on a large serving plate. Brush with puréed strawberries and spread on a layer of whipped topping. Place another cake layer over that and repeat until all cake, strawberries, and whipped topping are used. Garnish with the fresh strawberry slices.

NOTE: For best results, stack the layers with the cut side up because they'll hold the strawberries better. And for easy cutting, use a serrated knife.

# Crème Caramel

*6 to 8 servings*

*From north to south and east to west, almost everybody wants to claim this heavenly dessert as their own. All I know is, when I make it, everybody in my whole family claims it as his or her own!*

¾ cup sugar, divided
4 eggs
1 teaspoon vanilla extract
2 cups milk

Preheat the oven to 350°F. In a small nonstick skillet, stir ½ cup sugar over medium heat until completely melted and caramel-colored, about 6 minutes, stirring occasionally. Immediately pour the melted sugar into a 9-inch glass pie plate, coating the bottom of the plate. **(Be careful when working with the heated sugar; it is very hot.)** In a medium-sized bowl, beat the eggs with the vanilla. In a small bowl, combine the milk with the remaining ¼ cup sugar, then beat into the egg mixture. Pour over the caramelized sugar. Place the pie plate into a pan of hot water, with just enough water to go about halfway up the sides of the pie plate. Bake for 40 minutes or until a knife inserted into the center comes out clean. Let cool for 20 minutes, then cover and chill for 1 hour, or until ready to serve. Right before serving, invert the custard onto a 10- or 12-inch rimmed serving plate, so that the caramel sauce doesn't run off the plate.

NOTE: Be careful when inverting the pie plate. The best way is to place the serving plate upside down over the top of the pie pan and, holding the two together tightly, turn them over quickly. Then slowly remove the pie plate.

# Walnut Cake

*12 to 16 pieces*

*Greek bazaars are known for their great food and incredible desserts—and that's just where I got this recipe! The Greek woman who shared it with me spoke very little English, but her baking communicated smiles to everybody there.*

2 cups all-purpose flour
1 teaspoon baking powder
1 teaspoon baking soda
½ teaspoon ground cinnamon
½ cup (1 stick) butter, at room temperature
2¼ cups sugar, divided
2 eggs, lightly beaten
⅔ cup milk
1½ cups chopped walnuts
Grated rind of 1 lemon
1 cup water

Preheat the oven to 350°F. In a medium-sized bowl, combine the flour, baking powder, baking soda, and cinnamon; set aside. In a large bowl, cream the butter, then add 1 cup sugar and the eggs. Blend well and add the flour mixture alternately with the milk. Mix in the nuts and the lemon rind. Blend well and pour into a 9" × 13" baking pan that has been coated with nonstick baking spray. Bake for 40 to 45 minutes, or until a wooden toothpick inserted in the center comes out clean. Meanwhile, in a small saucepan, over medium heat, combine the remaining 1¼ cups sugar and the water and boil for 15 to 20 minutes just until it turns a light golden color. Pour the sauce over the cake while both are still warm. Turn off the oven and put the cake back into the warm oven for 5 minutes.

NOTE: This cake is best served warm. If you're not going to serve it right after baking, just pop it in the microwave (if it's in a microwaveable pan) on low power for about 1 minute or in a 250°F. oven for 10 to 15 minutes before serving.

# Tiramisù

*6 to 8 servings*

*Is there an Italian restaurant that isn't serving this Old World favorite today? If you dare to ask what's in it you'll probably hear that it's a secret. Well, not anymore—'cause you're gonna rush to make it at home!*

1 cup water
4 teaspoons instant coffee granules
¼ cup coffee-flavored liqueur
1 package (8 ounces) cream cheese, softened
¼ cup sour cream
2 tablespoons heavy cream
⅓ cup sugar
½ cup refrigerated egg substitute (the equivalent of 2 eggs)
2 cups frozen whipped topping, thawed
2 packages (3 ounces each) ladyfingers
1 teaspoon cocoa powder

In a small bowl, combine the water, instant coffee, and coffee liqueur; set aside. In a large bowl, blend the cream cheese, sour cream, and heavy cream until smooth. Add the sugar and egg substitute; mix well, then fold in the whipped topping. Using one package of ladyfingers, quickly dip the ladyfingers, one at a time, into the coffee mixture; use them to line the bottom of an 8-inch square glass baking dish. Spoon half of the cream mixture evenly over them. Quickly dip the second package of ladyfingers, one at a time, in the remaining coffee mixture; place them over the cream layer and top with the remaining cream mixture. Sprinkle with the cocoa powder, cover, and refrigerate for 3 to 4 hours or overnight.

# Swedish Pancakes

*18 to 20 pancakes*

*The French call them crêpes, Americans call them pancakes, and the Swedes call them perfect for rolling, folding, filling, or topping for anytime from breakfast and brunch through late-night treating!*

4 eggs
2 cups milk
1 cup all-purpose flour
2 tablespoons sugar
Dash of salt
4 tablespoons (½ stick) butter

Place all the ingredients except the butter in a blender. Blend just enough to combine the ingredients (don't overmix). In a large nonstick skillet or on a griddle, melt the butter over medium-low heat. Pour ¼ cup of batter per pancake into the skillet, cooking several pancakes at one time, but not overcrowding them. Flip the pancakes when the edges look like golden lace. Cook for just a bit longer, until the second side of the pancakes turns golden. (These don't take long to cook because the batter is thinner than regular pancake batter.) Repeat until all batter is used, adding the remaining butter to the pan as needed.

NOTE: These pancakes are thin, so they're easy to stack, roll, or fold—and they're good topped with maple or pancake syrup, canned pie filling, fresh or canned fruit, or even ice cream and chocolate or fruit sauce! Served plain or fancied-up, these are perfect for anytime you want something light and special!

# "Souper" Spice Cake

*10 to 12 servings*

*Spices were so important in "the olden days" that they were used for trading. Sure, they're still important today, but for their flavor more than their value. So when you're sinking your teeth into this dessert delight, think about how much each bite of this spice cake might have been worth years ago!*

INDIA
oh ye bahut
aeehaa hai!!
NEW DELHI

2 cups all-purpose flour
1⅓ cups granulated sugar
4 teaspoons baking powder
1 teaspoon baking soda
1½ teaspoons ground allspice
1 teaspoon ground cinnamon
1 can (10¾ ounces) condensed tomato soup
½ cup (1 stick) butter
2 eggs
¼ cup water

Preheat the oven to 350°F. Grease and flour two 8-inch cake pans or one 9" × 13" baking dish. Place all the ingredients in a blender and blend on low speed for about 1 minute. Blend on high for about 4 minutes, until well mixed. Pour the batter evenly into the cake pan(s) and bake for 35 to 40 minutes, or until a wooden toothpick inserted in the center comes out clean. Allow to cool before frosting and layering. If frosted, store cake in the refrigerator.

NOTE: Serve plain, or layered and topped with Cream Cheese Frosting (opposite) or whipped topping

# Cream Cheese Frosting

*enough for one two-layer cake*

1 package (8 ounces) cream cheese
1 cup (2 sticks) butter, softened
1 teaspoon vanilla extract
1 box (16 ounces) confectioners' sugar

In a large bowl, with an electric mixer, mix the cream cheese and butter. Add the vanilla and mix well. Gradually add the confectioners' sugar, continuing to mix until well combined. Top cooled cake(s). If making frosting in advance, cover and keep chilled. Let the frosting sit out at room temperature for 30 minutes before using.

# Crêpes Suzette

*10 to 12 crêpes*

*I remember the first time I had these in a fancy restaurant. I was so impressed because the taste was so special and because they were served flaming!!* **(I don't recommend that you flame these at home!)**

1 cup all-purpose flour
¼ teaspoon salt
1 tablespoon granulated sugar
1 tablespoon butter, melted
2 eggs
1½ cups milk
Vegetable oil for coating skillet
4 tablespoons (½ stick) butter
Juice and zest of 2 oranges
1 cup firmly packed brown sugar
2 tablespoons orange liqueur

In a medium-sized bowl, combine the flour, salt, granulated sugar, melted butter, and eggs; mix with an electric mixer for 1 to 2 minutes, then add the milk and beat until smooth. Brush a large nonstick skillet with oil and heat the skillet over medium-low heat. Pour ¼ cup of the batter into the skillet, tilting the skillet to evenly coat the bottom of the pan with the batter and cook for 1 minute per side, until the edges are brown and the crêpe has bubbled up. Remove crêpe to a heatproof platter and keep warm in a 200°F. oven. Repeat with the remaining batter, coating skillet with additional butter as needed. Then, in a small saucepan, combine the

4 tablespoons butter, orange juice, orange zest, and brown sugar. Heat over low heat for 6 to 8 minutes, then add the liqueur. Stir and remove from heat. Fold the crêpes in half and then in half the other way, making quarter-circles, and spoon a few tablespoons of the orange sauce over each crêpe. Serve immediately.

NOTE: These crêpes can be made several days in advance, layered with waxed paper, wrapped in plastic storage bags (to keep their freshness), and kept refrigerated. When ready to serve, make the sauce and prepare as above.

# "What a Pear!" Squares

*24 squares*

*There are so many apple desserts that I thought it was time for a change of pace. The taste of this one is a guaranteed winner!*

2 cups all-purpose flour
2 cups firmly packed brown sugar
½ cup (1 stick) butter
1 cup chopped blanched almonds
1 teaspoon ground cinnamon
1 teaspoon baking soda
½ teaspoon salt
1 cup plain yogurt
1 teaspoon vanilla extract
1 egg
1 can (16 ounces) pears, drained, dried, and cut into chunks

Preheat the oven to 350°F. In a large bowl, combine the flour, brown sugar, and butter; beat until crumbly. Stir in the nuts. Press 2¾ cups of the crumb mixture into the bottom of an ungreased 9" × 13" glass baking dish. Add the cinnamon, baking soda, salt, yogurt, vanilla, and egg to the remaining crumbly mixture; mix well. Stir in the pears. Spoon evenly over the crumb bottom and bake for 40 minutes or until a wooden toothpick inserted in the center comes out clean. Let cool for 1 hour.

NOTE: For a lower-fat dessert with the same big taste, substitute lowfat margarine for the butter and lowfat yogurt for regular yogurt.

# English Tea Pastries

*16 pieces*

*It's tea time! I love the British tradition of having tea and cakes every after-noon. How 'bout making these easy pastries for your own tea time?*

1 package (8 ounces) refrigerator crescent rolls (eight rolls
per package)
3 tablespoons strawberry or raspberry fruit preserves or jam
1 tablespoon butter, melted
1 tablespoon chopped blanched almonds
1 tablespoon confectioners' sugar

Preheat the oven to 375°F. Separate the crescent rolls into indi-vidual triangles. Cut each triangle in half lengthwise, making 16 long triangles. Spread about ½ teaspoon of preserves over each triangle. Roll each triangle from the wide end to the point, and place on a cookie sheet that has been coated with nonstick baking spray. Brush with the butter and sprinkle with the chopped nuts. Bake for 15 to 17 minutes, or until golden. When cool, sprinkle with the confectioners' sugar and serve.

NOTE: These are quick throw-together treats that are perfect for dunking in tea—and coffee, too. And remember, make as many as you need by using more packages of crescent rolls (and every-thing else, too!).

OOH IT'S SO GOOD!!™ - ENGLAND ENGLAND LONDON

# Romanoff Sauce

*6 to 7 cups*

*If you want to show off with a recipe that's been passed down from generation to generation, here's the answer!*

1½ cups water
6 egg yolks
1 cup sugar
⅓ cup cocktail sherry or fruit-flavored liqueur
1 container (12 ounces) frozen whipped topping, thawed

Place the water in the bottom of a double boiler. Bring to a boil over high heat. Reduce the heat to low and, in the top of the double boiler, combine the egg yolks and sugar. Stir constantly for 5 to 6 minutes until the sugar dissolves and the mixture begins to thicken. Remove from the heat and add the sherry. Let cool for 20 to 30 minutes. Place the whipped topping in a large bowl and fold in the cooled egg mixture until evenly combined.

NOTE: Serve over hulled strawberries, drained canned peaches, or fresh blueberries. If you don't have a double boiler, you can use 2 pots (one smaller than the other) and nest one inside the other.

# Mini-Elephant Ears

*18 to 20 servings*

*In pastry shops all over Europe you can find these delicate, crisp pastries that have been rolled in cinnamon and sugar. Hooray! Now they're easy to make at home.*

2 frozen puff pastry sheets (from a 17¼-ounce package),
slightly thawed
2 teaspoons ground cinnamon
⅔ cup sugar
1 egg, beaten

Preheat the oven to 400°F. On a lightly floured surface, with a rolling pin, roll out each pastry sheet to a 12-inch square. In a small bowl, combine the cinnamon and sugar. Brush the pastry sheets with the beaten egg and sprinkle 3 tablespoons of the cinnamon mixture evenly over the top of each sheet. Roll one side of the pastry sheet into the middle, then roll the other side to meet it in the middle, forming a scroll. Cut ½-inch slices across the scrolls. Dip one cut side of each slice into the cinnamon mixture and lay them dipped side up on a cookie sheet that has been lightly coated with nonstick baking spray. Bake for 14 to 17 minutes, then let cool for 5 minutes and remove from the pan.

NOTE: These should be stored in an airtight container or cookie jar. They shouldn't be refrigerated or frozen.

# Almost-Belgian Chocolate Mousse

*6 to 8 servings*

*I'm not sure if it's true, but I've heard that the first chocolate mousse was made from rich Belgian chocolate. Well, since most of us don't usually have real Belgian chocolate on hand, I've come up with a quick, easy way to copy those incomparable tastes.*

1 cup (6 ounces) semisweet chocolate chips
1 pint heavy cream
⅛ teaspoon instant coffee granules
1 teaspoon water

In a small saucepan, melt the chocolate over low heat until smooth, stirring constantly. Set aside until slightly cooled. Place the heavy cream in a large bowl and beat with an electric mixer until light and fluffy. Gently fold in the chocolate. In a cup, dissolve the instant coffee in the water, then gently fold into the chocolate mixture. Cover and refrigerate until ready to serve.

NOTE: For an extra-special way to serve this, spoon it into individual serving cups and top with some additional whipped cream. It's also nice to add a European touch by grating a bit of a chocolate bar over the top of each.

# Floating Swedish Cream

*4 to 6 servings*

*Most people think that all Old World foods are hearty and heavy. Not true! This recipe is as Old World and as light as can be!*

1 pint half-and-half
1 envelope (¼ ounce) unflavored gelatin
¾ cup sugar
1 pint sour cream
½ teaspoon vanilla extract
½ teaspoon almond extract
1 can (16 ounces) sliced peaches, drained

In a small saucepan, over low heat, heat the half-and-half, gelatin, and sugar, stirring frequently for 8 to 10 minutes, until all the sugar is dissolved. Do not allow to boil. Remove from the heat and cool for 5 minutes. With a wire whisk, beat in the sour cream and the vanilla and almond extracts. Pour into a 9-inch glass pie plate and chill for 2 to 3 hours. Top with the sliced peaches.

NOTE: This is great as is, or you might want to top it with any kind of fresh fruit that's in season.

MR. FOOD®'S OLD WORLD
OOH IT'S SO GOOD!!™
COOKING MADE EASY

# Zesty Ricotta Pie

*8 servings*

*One taste and you'll know why all my Italian friends try to keep this recipe a secret!*

1 container (15 ounces) ricotta cheese
½ cup sugar
1 teaspoon lemon zest
3 eggs
1 teaspoon vanilla extract
One 9-inch (6 ounces) graham cracker pie crust
3 tablespoons raspberry preserves, melted
1 tablespoon chopped blanched almonds

Preheat the oven to 400°F. In a medium-sized bowl, with an electric mixer, combine the ricotta cheese, sugar, lemon zest, eggs, and vanilla. Pour the mixture into the pie crust. Bake for 7 minutes, reduce the temperature to 300°F., and bake for an additional 55 to 65 minutes or until the center is set. Remove from the oven and cool for 15 to 20 minutes. Spread the top with the melted raspberry preserves and chopped almonds.

NOTE: Where do you get lemon zest? Just rub the skin of a cleaned lemon over a grater and you've got fresh lemon zest!

# European Chocolate Cookies

*about 2½ dozen cookies*

*Let your taste buds travel to Europe while you and your family travel back and forth to the cookie jar.*

1½ cups semisweet chocolate chips, divided
1 square (1 ounce) unsweetened baking chocolate
1 tablespoon unsalted butter
⅓ cup firmly packed dark brown sugar
1 egg
1 tablespoon water
1 teaspoon vanilla extract
2 tablespoons all-purpose flour
⅛ teaspoon baking powder
1 cup coarsely chopped walnuts

In the top of a double boiler, or in a stainless-steel bowl set over a saucepan of simmering water, melt ½ cup chocolate chips, the unsweetened chocolate, and the butter over simmering water until smooth and well blended. Transfer the chocolate mixture to a medium-sized bowl and let cool slightly. Blend the brown sugar, egg, water, and vanilla into the slightly cooled chocolate mixture. Stir in the flour and baking powder until well mixed. Stir in the remaining 1 cup chocolate chips and the nuts. (The batter will be very sticky.) Cover and refrigerate for at least 1½ hours, or overnight. Preheat the oven to 350°F. Line 2 cookie sheets with aluminum foil. Drop the batter by teaspoonfuls onto the prepared cookie sheets. Bake for 13 to 15 minutes, or until the cookies are firm to the touch, reversing the position of the trays once during baking. Remove the cookie sheets from the oven and place on wire racks. Allow the cookies to cool completely before removing from the foil.

NOTE: Store in an airtight container to maintain the scrumptious flavor!

# Old-Fashioned Bread Pudding

*10 to 12 servings*

*I don't think there could be any more successful way to use leftovers than in bread pudding. We're lucky... our ancestors couldn't afford to waste anything, and this was the perfect way to use their stale bread. I love it so much that I try to plan on having leftover bread.*

1 pound day-old bread (10 to 12 slices), torn into 1-inch pieces
2 cups warm water
3 eggs
½ pint heavy cream
½ cup raisins
1 teaspoon vanilla extract
¾ cup granulated sugar
1 teaspoon salt
½ teaspoon ground cinnamon
½ cup confectioners' sugar
1 tablespoon plus 2 teaspoons whiskey

Preheat the oven to 350°F. In a large bowl, toss together the bread pieces and water, soaking the bread. In a small bowl, beat the eggs, then stir in the heavy cream. Add to the soaked bread along with the raisins, vanilla, granulated sugar, salt, and cinnamon; stir until well combined. Place in an 8-inch square glass baking dish that has been coated with nonstick baking spray. Bake for 60 to 65 minutes or until puffy and firm in the center. Meanwhile, in another small bowl, combine the confectioners' sugar and whiskey, stirring until smooth. Remove the finished pudding from the oven and, while still warm, top with the whiskey glaze.

NOTE: This should be served warm, so if not serving it right from the oven, then cool, cover, and store in the refrigerator. Just before serving, reheat the pudding, covered, in a 300°F. oven for about 15 minutes, *then* top with the glaze.

# Orange Poppy Seed Cookies

*3½ to 4 dozen cookies*

*I have to thank my wife for these because she took a basic Old World sugar cookie recipe and fancied it up. Wow! Make way for Mrs. Food!*

¾ cup (1½ sticks) butter, softened
1 cup sugar
1 egg
1 teaspoon vanilla extract
⅛ teaspoon salt
2 tablespoons poppy seeds
½ teaspoon orange extract
2 cups all-purpose flour

In a large bowl, beat together the butter and sugar with an electric beater. Add the egg, vanilla, and salt; beat until smooth. Stir in the poppy seeds and orange extract. Stir in the flour and knead lightly until a soft dough forms. Divide the dough in half, then wrap each half in waxed paper to form a cylinder about 1½ inches in diameter. Flatten the sides of the wrapped dough to form a rectangular shape. Refrigerate the dough until firm, about 2 hours. Preheat the oven to 350°F. Cut the dough into ¼-inch slices and arrange on cookie sheets that have been coated with nonstick baking spray. Bake for 12 to 15 minutes. Remove cookies from the cookie sheets while still slightly warm.

# South of the Border Doughnuts

*3 to 3½ dozen doughnuts*

*The Mexicans call these* buñuelos, *and they're perfect for an after-siesta (or anytime) nibble.*

⅔ cup sugar, divided
1 teaspoon ground cinnamon
¼ cup (½ stick) butter, softened
2 eggs
1 teaspoon vanilla extract
1¾ cups all-purpose flour, divided (or more as needed)
2 teaspoons baking powder
1 teaspoon salt
¼ cup milk
Vegetable oil for frying

In a shallow pan, combine ⅓ cup sugar and the cinnamon; set aside. In a medium-sized bowl, using an electric mixer, cream together the butter and remaining ⅓ cup sugar until creamy. Add the eggs and vanilla, blending well. Mix in 1 cup of the flour, the baking powder, and salt; mix well and blend in the milk. Add the remaining flour and mix to make a soft dough. Turn out onto a floured surface and knead for 1 to 2 minutes or until the dough is smooth, kneading in more flour if the dough is still too sticky to handle. With a rolling pin, roll out the dough to ¼-inch thickness, flouring the surface and rolling pin lightly if the dough sticks. Cut the dough with a 2-inch round cookie cutter. In a heavy skillet or Dutch oven, heat 2 inches of oil over medium heat, until hot but not burning or smoking (350°F.). Fry six 2-inch rounds at a time for 1½ to 2 minutes, until puffy and golden, turning often with tongs. Drain on paper towels and toss in the sugar and cinnamon coating mix while still hot.

NOTE: These should look like puffy fried dough balls.

# Chocolate-Dipped Walnut Wedges

*about 32 cookies*

*I did borrow this favorite European recipe from my cookie cookbook—but only because it's so popular and it fits so perfectly here. If you haven't tried it yet, give it a try now.*

1¼ cups (about 6 ounces) shelled walnuts
1¼ cups all-purpose flour plus extra for dusting
¾ cup sugar
10 tablespoons (1¼ sticks) butter
¾ cup (4 ounces) semisweet chocolate chips
1 tablespoon vegetable shortening

Preheat the oven to 350°F. In a food processor, finely grind the walnuts, 1¼ cups flour, and sugar, using the cutting blade. Add the butter and blend until well mixed. Coat two 8-inch round cake pans with nonstick baking spray and dust lightly with flour. Press half of the dough into each pan, evenly covering the pan bottoms. With a small knife, score each pan of dough into 16 wedges, being careful not to cut through the dough. Bake in the middle of the oven for 20 minutes or until golden brown. While the shortbread is still warm, cut through the scored lines and allow to cool in the pans on a wire rack. In a small heavy saucepan, melt the chocolate chips and shortening, stirring until smooth. Dip the points of the cooled shortbread wedges into the chocolate mixture, coating them halfway, allowing any excess chocolate to drip off. Put the dipped wedges on a wire rack over waxed paper and allow to set.

# Danish Almond Loaf

*8 to 10 servings*

*Denmark has a reputation for being a great place for dessert lovers, especially almond lovers. (That's 'cause they're grown right there!)*

⅔ cup butter
1¼ cups sugar
3 eggs
½ cup blanched almonds, finely ground
½ teaspoon almond extract
⅛ teaspoon ground cinnamon
1⅓ cups all-purpose flour
1 teaspoon baking powder
⅓ cup blanched almonds, coarsely chopped

Preheat the oven to 325°F. In a large bowl, beat the butter and sugar until soft and fluffy. Gradually beat in the eggs, one at a time, until a fine mixture forms, about 1 to 2 minutes. Add the finely ground almonds, almond extract, and cinnamon and mix thoroughly. Blend in the flour and baking powder. Sprinkle the coarsely chopped almonds into a 9" × 5" loaf pan that has been coated with nonstick baking spray. Spoon the batter over the almonds and bake for 55 to 60 minutes or until a wooden toothpick inserted in the center comes out clean.

NOTE: Serve this with dollops of whipped cream or a dusting of confectioners' sugar.

# European Wine Biscuits

*about 5 dozen biscuits*

*Wine in biscuits?! Sure, you've heard of cooking chicken, meat, fish, and even cakes with wine, and now it's the secret ingredient that makes these European biscuits so special!*

1 cup (2 sticks) butter, softened
1 cup sweet red wine
1½ cups granulated sugar
1 tablespoon plus 1 teaspoon baking powder
1 teaspoon salt
4 cups all-purpose flour
1 teaspoon vanilla extract
1 cup confectioners' sugar

Preheat the oven to 350°F. In a large bowl, combine the butter, wine, and granulated sugar until well blended. Add the baking powder, salt, flour, and vanilla, mixing until well blended. With a rolling pin, roll out the dough onto a floured board to ¼-inch thickness. Cut out the cookies with a 2-inch cookie cutter. Place on cookie sheets that have been coated with nonstick baking spray. Bake for 15 to 18 minutes. Let cookies cool for 5 minutes. Shake a few cookies at a time in a plastic bag with the confectioners' sugar until well coated. Repeat until all the cookies are coated.

NOTE: Any wine will work in this recipe, but I prefer to use a sweet red wine!!

# Tortoni

*12 to 14 cups*

*No, no ... put away the ice cream maker and put down the car keys. You don't have to go to an import store to pick up these ingredients. It's as easy as mixing and freezing—and before you know it, you'll be a kitchen hero!*

1 quart (2½ cups) vanilla ice cream
1½ cups frozen whipped topping, thawed
1½ teaspoons almond extract
½ cup plus 2 tablespoons chopped blanched almonds
6 to 7 maraschino cherries, cut in half

Line 12 to 14 muffin cups with paper baking cups. In a large bowl, soften the ice cream (see Note). Fold in the whipped topping and mix well. Add the almond extract and the ½ cup almonds; mix well again. Place about ⅓ cup of the ice cream mixture into each muffin cup. Sprinkle with the remaining almonds. Cover the muffin cups and place in the freezer for 2 to 3 hours. Just before serving, garnish each with a maraschino cherry half.

NOTE: To soften ice cream, break it up in a mixing bowl and stir with a wooden spoon. **Do not let the ice cream reach the melting point.** Why not change the rules and substitute other ice cream flavors for the vanilla? It might not be truly Italian that way, but it'll still be good . . . and different!

# Apple Kuchen

*15 servings*

*When I started this chapter, this was the first recipe I made. My cousin shared her recipe with me and I took a few shortcuts. And after I tasted it, I knew I was going to really enjoy making all these Old World desserts. Did you? I hope so!*

1 package (20 ounces) refrigerated sugar cookie dough
3 apples, peeled and cored, sliced ¼-inch thick (2 cups)
2 tablespoons lemon juice
¼ cup plus 2 tablespoons sugar
1 teaspoon ground cinnamon
½ cup all-purpose flour
2 tablespoons (¼ stick) butter

Preheat the oven to 350°F. Press the cookie dough into a 9" × 13" baking pan, completely covering the bottom of the pan. In a medium-sized bowl, mix the apples with the lemon juice, 2 tablespoons sugar, and the cinnamon and distribute evenly over the cookie dough. In a small bowl, combine the ¼ cup sugar, the flour, and butter and mix with a fork until crumbly. Sprinkle over the apple mixture and bake for 30 minutes or until the top is golden brown.

NOTE: Make sure you've got some vanilla ice cream on hand when this comes out of the oven. What a match . . . it's a taste worth remembering!

# Index

tres leches, 212
Turkish pilaf, 162
Tuscany bread salad, 46

Ukrainian garlic-crusted liver, 90

veal:
German-style stuffed cutlets,
80–81
Oscar, award-winning, 108
tied-up breast of, 100–101
vegetable(s), 187–205
toss-together salad, 194
*see also specific vegetables*

walnut:
cake, 222–223
chocolate-dipped wedges, 244
"What a pear!" squares, 230
windmill pasta, 184
wine biscuits, European, 246
wined and dined chicken, 130–131
wrapped-up Brie, 16

Yorkshire pudding, winning, 48

zucchini:
all-star, 191
minty Indian, 199